American Heroes of World War II

True Stories of Individual Bravery from the Battlefields of World War II

By Alex Viner

Table of Contents

Introduction

We have faith that future generations will know here, in the middle of the twentieth century, there came a time when men of good will found a way to unite, and produce, and fight to destroy the forces of ignorance, and intolerance, and slavery, and war. –Franklin D. Roosevelt

The impact of World War II reverberated around all corners of the globe and forced acts of bravery from people from all walks of life. This book will take a look at the actions of a diverse group of Americans who rolled their sleeves up when their country needed them despite the personal cost.

From the beaches of Normandy to the dense jungles of New Guinea, the Allied forces fought the Axis powers in a fight for power, control, and ultimately freedom—a fight that would be, and hopefully will be, the most destructive battle the world will ever see.

Over time, crumbled cities were rebuilt. In the United States, Veterans Day gives thanks to those who have served their country on November 11th, and Memorial Day is celebrated on the last Monday of May, to pay respect to those who gave their lives for our freedom.

While notable American names such as decorated Medal of Honor recipient Audie Murphy and future Presidents John F. Kennedy and Dwight D. Eisenhower have rightly received public acclaim, there are many other American heroes who we are in danger of forgetting about—heroes like aerial ace Phil Rasmussen, tank-riding William H. Wilbur, and ambulance driver turned spy Virginia Hall. In this book, we'll explore the heroic actions of 28 lesser-known American heroes who rose to the occasion to influence key battles, shape pivotal campaigns, and ultimately, ensure the victory of the allied forces.

The heroes featured are no different than you and me.

They were ordinary people who were taken from their lives as factory workers, mechanics, and construction workers, leaving behind their parents, spouses, and children. These people were brave enough to grab the mantel with both hands, performing truly extraordinary acts of bravery so that once the dust settled, the bullets cooled, and the blood dried, the future of their loved ones and their country was secure.

Welcome to *American Heroes of World War II* and the true stories of individual bravery displayed throughout America's bloodiest battles.

Chapter 1:

Doris Miller

United States Navy, Pearl Harbor, 1941

It wasn't hard. I just pulled the trigger, and she worked fine. I had watched the others with these guns. I guess I fired her for about fifteen minutes. I think I got one of those Jap planes. They were diving pretty close to us. –Doris Miller

Background of the Hero

While Doris Miller may not think his actions should be considered "hard," the actions he took on December 7, 1941, saved countless lives and rightfully earned him a place in our collection of American heroes.

Before he was a hero, however, he was a young boy named Doris Miller. Born on October 12, 1919, his parents, Connery and Henrietta Miller, were both sharecroppers from Waco, Texas. I'm sure neither of them could have had any idea that the tender baby they'd been blessed with would grow into the first black Navy Cross recipient.

Doris was the third of four sons and was actually expected to be a daughter, with the midwife who delivered him suggesting his name because of that fact.

As a young boy, Doris helped his family alongside his brothers, cooking hot meals and helping with the laundry, two skills that would later see him become a valuable member of the Navy.

His journey wasn't a straightforward one, though. After rising to acclaim as the star fullback at Waco's Alexander James Moore High School, Doris' sporting achievements were papering over the cracks of poor academic performance.

Forced to repeat the eighth grade in 1937, at the age of 17, Doris unfortunately failed it again and ultimately dropped out of high school completely. Having filled his time working on his family's farm, squirrel hunting, and completing a taxidermy course, Doris needed a path to follow.

He made his first attempt to give back to his country around this time when he applied to join the Civilian Conservation Corps, a voluntary program for unemployed men seeking to help conserve and develop the country's natural resources, but he was sadly turned down. Doris put his 6-foot-3-inch and 200-plus-pound frame to work on his family's farm and made another now crucial decision in his journey: taking a job as a cook in a local restaurant during the Great Depression.

Less than a month before Doris' 20th birthday, a recruiting station in Dallas, Texas, enlisted him into the United States Navy and sealed his fate.

Doris was impressive throughout his naval training and was quick to receive the rank of Mess Attendant Third Class from the Norfolk Naval Training Station in Virginia, which had been tasked with hammering him into shape. His first temporary assignment saw him set sail on the *USS Pyro* in 1939 before he was assigned permanent duty less than two months later on the ill-fated *USS West Virginia.*

Doris had no interest in doing the bare minimum. He supplemented his primary duties of serving food and bussing tables in the Junior Officers' Mess Hall by volunteering as a room steward, a role that would require him to shine shoes, make beds, collect laundry, and wake duty officers up in the morning.

He was climbing the ranks and was promoted to mess attendant second class just a year later, simultaneously earning the respect of his peers by winning his division in a heavyweight boxing competition held on the ship.

The Heroic Act

The morning of December 7, 1941, appeared to be an ordinary one for Doris. Having served breakfast, he set about collecting the soiled laundry of junior officers, a task that he was right in the middle of when the *West Virginia* was brutally rocked by the first of a seven-torpedo volley sent by the Japanese aircraft carrier, *Akagi.* Doris' first port of call was to rush to his assigned battle station, an anti-aircraft battery magazine in the middle of the ship. However, when he got there, he realized it had already been reduced to rubble.

Surrounded by chaos and fear, rather than run away from danger, Doris ran straight toward it, heading to "Times Square" on the ship's starboard, where he immediately put his hulking frame to work—just as he had on his family's farm—to carry injured sailors from the line of fire.

Doris didn't realize this at the time, but one of the sailors who would need his help more than most was Captain Mervin S. Bennion. Bennion had been seriously wounded by shrapnel from the first torpedo and was left with a gash in his abdomen between three and four inches wide that put him in grave danger of losing his life.

When the ship's commander, D.C. Johnson, rushed past "Times Square" en route to rescue his captain, he saw Doris Miller's strength and bravery in rescuing his fellow men.

Johnson would later describe Doris as "very powerfully built" and with the means to carry the captain safely below deck (Aiken, 2001).

Doris helped Johnson carry their captain, putting himself in the line of fire to brave the damaged bridge and eventually safely transferring him to a sheltered spot behind the conning tower.

A deadly concoction of fire and smoke made their plan to move their captain below deck impossible, and a new plan was hatched in the heat of battle. They planned to move him to the safety of the navigation bridge in a cot, which was a daring move with a very slim chance of success—but the only move they had.

To complete that move, however, they needed a distraction from the planes screaming overhead that would provide them with the time they needed to build the necessary cot.

Covered in blood and sweat and struggling to see through the thick smoke that had engulfed the ship, Doris was more than happy to provide such a distraction.

With the screeching of the "banshee death wail" diving down on them from above, Doris accompanied a couple of soldiers to two unmanned anti-aircraft machine guns on the conning tower so that he could help feed ammunition into them.

With very little training, no experience operating such a weapon in the field of battle, and the sheer determination to save his fellow Americans, Doris absolutely let rip.

With his captain losing pints of blood below him, Doris thrust himself into a post on the starboard gun and directly into the line of fire. He rattled shells at the Japanese bombers overhead until he'd completely exhausted his body of energy and the weapon of ammunition.

Doris' sharp shooting destroyed at least two planes that day, but unfortunately, the distraction he helped provide wasn't enough time to find his captain the cot he desperately needed.

An oil fire shortly erupted on the boat deck, but despite the captain's orders to head below, Doris returned with his comrades and made one last attempt to save his captain's life.

The men were able to lift their fallen captain up out of the smoke on the navigation bridge just seconds before it was engulfed by a raging inferno. Then Doris set about fighting the inferno with a fire hose alongside two other soldiers. Doris' heroic efforts would sadly be in vain when the captain perished from his wounds, and the Japanese were far from finished.

A further two armor-piercing bombs tore through *West Virginia's* deck, and five more torpedoes ripped through her port side.

With the ship's crew frantically working to counter-flood the ship and prevent her from capsizing in the face of deadly explosions and uncontrollable fires, Doris wiped the blood and oil from his eyes and began dragging his fellow injured men through oily water to the quarterdeck, saving countless lives.

By the culmination of the attack, the *West Virginia* had sunk in the shallow waters of Pearl Harbor, and 132 of its crew had perished, with a further 52 injured (Miller, 2019). But there is no doubt that if Doris hadn't been aboard that day, those numbers would have been much greater.

The Aftermath of the Act

Doris' military career continued after his heroics on that fateful day, and it took him just another year to be promoted again, this time to mess attendant first class.

Unfortunately, the racial discrimination that was rife across the country at the time meant that Doris wasn't initially recognized for his heroics. He was shunned to such an extent, in fact, that he was excluded from a war bond tour that was held for white war heroes in the United States, celebrating the bravery that was shown during the Pearl Harbor attack.

The outcry was so severe that the newspaper, *Pittsburgh Courier*, led the charge for Doris to be allowed to join the tour. On the 25th of July, they even ran a damning photo of Doris with the headline, "He fought... Keeps Mop," alongside a photo of a white survivor of Pearl Harbor receiving their accolades ("*He Fought... Keeps Mop,*" 1942).

The groundswell became so great that it eventually led to Doris being recognized on a war bond tour later that year. In the months that followed, Doris was empowered by the opportunity to give a presentation to the first graduating class of black sailors from Great Lakes Naval Training Station and was even featured personally on a Navy recruitment poster in 1943!

Doris' career continued on a steady incline throughout 1943, and he was promoted to cook third class.

Doris would ultimately perish in 1943 at the age of just 24 when he was a member of the crew of *USS Liscome Bay* that was struck by the torpedo of a Japanese submarine. Of the crew that included more than 900 men, only 272 survived (Miller, 2019).

Doris' death was officially declared by the United States Navy on November 25, 1944.

A Lasting Legacy

Doris left a lasting legacy that is still felt to this very day.

Having been denied a Medal of Honor because of the color of his skin, Doris would later be awarded the Navy Cross by Admiral Chester Nimitz on May 27, 1942. His citation reads:

> For distinguished devotion to duty, extraordinary courage, and disregard for his own personal safety during the attack on the Fleet in Pearl Harbor, Territory of Hawaii, by Japanese forces on December 7, 1941.
>
> While at the side of his Captain on the bridge, Miller, despite enemy strafing and bombing and in the face of a serious fire, assisted in moving his Captain, who had

> been mortally wounded, to a place of greater safety and later manned and operated a machine gun directed at enemy Japanese attacking aircraft until ordered to leave the bridge. (Cook Third Class Doris Miller's Navy Cross Citation, 2020)

Doris was also awarded a clutch of other military medals for his actions that day, including (Miller, 2017):

- Purple Heart
- American Campaign Medal
- Good Conduct Medal
- American Defense Service Medal
- Asiatic-Pacific Campaign Medal
- Combat Action Ribbon

Doris was represented on the big screen in both *Pearl Harbor* and *Midway,* as well as having his story dramatized in a number of radio shows.

A whole host of schools, memorials, and community centers have been named in his honor, as well as military premises and vehicles, such as the mess hall where his military career started and a destroyer escort.

In 2010, Doris was one of only four sailors honored on a U.S. postage stamp, and the *USS Doris Miller*, a nuclear-powered aircraft carrier, is scheduled for commissioning in 2032, making Miller the first African American enlisted sailor to have an aircraft carrier named after him.

In 1943, the Doris Miller Foundation (now the American Heritage and Freedom Award) was established. The annual award champions outstanding individuals or groups that work in the field of race relations.

Perhaps his most crowning achievement, however, was the spotlight his achievements shone on the racial disparity of the time and the startling lack of credit that one's heroic actions could receive simply because of the color of their skin.

Chapter 2:

Vernon Baker

United States Army, Castle Aghinolfi, 1945

Give respect before you expect it. Treat people the way you want to be treated. Remember the mission. Set the example. Keep going. –Vernon Baker

Background of the Hero

Vernon Baker was born on December 17, 1919, in the city of Cheyenne, Wyoming. He was the youngest of three children, but his parents would sadly perish in a car accident when he was just four years old.

Rather than see the children be shipped off to an orphanage, Vernon's grandparents stepped in and raised Vernon and his two older sisters. He became incredibly close to his grandfather, who worked as a railroad worker.

Vernon spent lots of time with his grandfather, learning to hunt, which was a vital means of feeding the family. From a young age, he was more than willing to help shoulder the responsibility of sourcing wild game and rabbit for the rest of the family—a responsibility that crucially required him to hone his skills with a rifle, which he would need later.

Perhaps even more crucial than the rifle skills his grandfather taught him were his interpersonal skills. Vernon was taught the value of being forgiving and thoughtful. He was encouraged to always use his brain rather than his fists and warned that hate would only bring destruction (Olsen, 2010).

The relationship with his grandfather was so profound that Vernon considered him the most influential figure in his life (*First Lieutenant Vernon J. Baker*, n.d.).

Sadly, his relationship with his grandmother was extremely strained, resulting in the opposite of the stability that his grandfather had provided.

His grandmother was bound to a wheelchair because of severe arthritis, and things became so strained between the pair that Vernon would spend short stints at the Boys Town orphanage in Nebraska to find reprieve.

Vernon's peers at the orphanage found themselves in the presence of a softly spoken and well-mannered boy who had little time for bullies. He consistently defended those smaller and weaker than him and stood up for what he believed in.

He had a good heart and appeared to be unflappable. Perhaps that was because of the strength his grandfather had instilled in him or maybe it was simply the strength that one has to find after facing death at such a tender age.

Regardless of the pieces that formed Vernon's early stature, his cool head provided the foundation he needed to prevent the tension with his grandmother from hurting his performance at high school.

Having graduated in 1939, Vernon found himself at the well-trodden fork in the road faced by all high school graduates and pondered what was next.

It should come as no surprise that Vernon turned to his grandfather once more in this period and soon found himself working alongside him as a railroad porter. Vernon hated the job and wanted out, but it wasn't until his grandfather passed away from cancer over the Christmas period of 1939 that he took the brave step of quitting.

Perhaps Vernon didn't want to let his grandfather down and seem ungrateful for the opportunity. Or was another death in the life of a young man who had already felt such loss the kick that he needed to truly seek his purpose?

Regardless, it would only take Vernon another year of working odd jobs before he homed in on his goal: He wanted to fight for his country. In an incredible indictment of the state of the world at the time, Vernon found himself turned away by the first recruiter that he approached and told that there wasn't any room for "you people" (Olsen, 2010).

Thankfully, cooler heads prevailed, and when Vernon approached a different recruiter the following week, he was accepted. Despite requesting to join as a quartermaster, Vernon was recruited as an infantry member. He kept quiet for fear of hurting his chances of admission.

Vernon was assigned to the 1st Battalion, 370th Infantry Regiment, 92nd Infantry Division, following his basic training at Camp Walters in Texas. Despite completing his training and proving himself as a more-than-worthy member of his division, things were going to be far from easy.

He faced racial discrimination throughout his tenure that prevented him from using the front entrance of an officer's club in Fort Huachuca, despite the fact that even German prisoners of war were allowed access to it. Undeterred, Vernon completed Officer Candidate School in 1943 and was subsequently commissioned as a second lieutenant.

Discrimination wasn't his only problem, though. He was also targeted by African Americans who felt he was too smart and were jealous and resentful of the way that he was rising through the ranks. At one point, Vernon was even jumped by three black soldiers and whipped relentlessly.

It wasn't until 1944, with the United States Army struggling for numbers and facing increasing pressure from the black community, that they finally formed the all-black 92nd Infantry Division. Vernon was shipped to Naples in Italy, and it didn't take long for him to earn the respect of those around him with his heart, fighting spirit, and skill with a rifle that his beloved grandfather had afforded him.

After taking a bullet to the arm in October, Vernon found himself hospitalized near Pisa for two months. Eager to return to the battlefield, he was promptly patched up and returned to the fight in December, where he found his Allied brothers still pinned down by the artillery batteries, bunkers, and machine gun nests along the Gothic Line. The line stretched the width of northern Italy, allowing Axis forces to weave themselves into the natural fortifications of the Apennine Mountains, posing an incredibly daunting task for the Allies.

Perhaps the most daunting fortification that the Axis had established was the 15th-century castle, Aghinolfi. The castle was positioned advantageously on a hilltop, which made capturing it extremely difficult.

Despite the difficulty that the capture posed, it was vital in relinquishing the control that the Germans had gained of the western end of the Gothic Line. The Allies' desperate attempts to achieve this relinquishment were formulated via a series of daylight attacks that unfortunately resulted in multiple unsuccessful raids and the slaughter of many Allied soldiers.

Vernon's detachment was held in reserve, meaning that he was essentially helpless to watch as other detachments tried and failed to capture the stronghold. One can only imagine the concoction of fear and anger he felt as he watched his battalion dwindle in numbers with little chance of success.

It was in the early spring that Vernon's time would finally come, and he was sure to make the most of it.

The Heroic Act

It was before dawn on April 5 when Vernon and his heavy weapons platoon managed to daringly slip through barbed wire, German defenses, and minefields to get within sight of the castle. With the stronghold within touching distance and an opportunity to deliver a decisive blow to the Germans that had appeared impossible throughout the prior months, Vernon used his brain just as his grandfather had taught him.

While finding an effective position to set up a machine gun, something caught his eye. He noticed the glistening of two metal cylinders through an ominous slit in a hill, an observation post that was sure to cut Vernon and his men down once they became aware that they'd managed to tiptoe through the minefield.

Vernon dropped to his belly and crawled to the opening, slid his M-1 machine gun through the slit, and emptied his entire clip, killing the two oblivious occupants and rendering the post utterly ineffective.

While scouring the area, Vernon then spotted a well-camouflaged machine gun nest. Again, he patiently crawled his way over to the nest, but this time, he found a crew of German soldiers eating their breakfast—a testament to just how confident they were that the Allies wouldn't make it so deep behind enemy lines. Vernon unloaded his machine gun once more and killed all present in the nest.

As he started to return to his platoon, they were joined by the commander of another Allied detachment, finally catching up to Vernon's rapid advance. Before the pair could exchange pleasantries, they were surprised by a German soldier who tossed a grenade in their direction.

The grenade failed to explode; Vernon had got lucky. Rather than count his blessings, though, he sank two bullets into the enemy soldier as he tried to return to the sanctity of the trench that he'd sprung up from.

The enemy that had so nearly snatched Vernon's life was dead by his hand, but far from resting on his laurels, Vernon recognized the opportunity to infiltrate the trench that he was returning to and pressed on alone. He crept down into the dugout with the earthy smell penetrating his nostrils and gun gripped tightly.

Soon, he was confronted by a concealed entrance of a hideout. He surprised those inside by blowing through the entrance with the toss of a hand grenade, gunning down the dirt-stained German soldier that emerged in the aftermath.

Before pressing on, Vernon tossed a second grenade down into the dugout and raced in with his submachine gun, following the explosion to tear bullets through two more soldiers.

The dugout was no longer a threat to the Allies, but when Vernon pulled himself back up out of the trench, he was met by the horrific sight of heavy Allied casualties. His men were dying, and his submachine gun was no match for the crackling symphony of mortar and machine gun fire that was raining down on them.

Vernon watched helplessly as 25 soldiers were cut down by around two-thirds and desperately called for artillery support. His calls were completely disregarded by American officers, who scoffed at the idea that they were so deep in enemy territory, leaving them completely exposed to the bombardment.

Even in the heat of battle, the racial discrimination that had plagued Vernon's life would resurface when a white commander evacuated under the guise of rousing reinforcements but left the all-black platoon as lambs to the slaughter when he instead reported that they'd all perished.

The reinforcements failed to arrive and he was running out of options. Vernon's captain ordered that the remaining men withdraw in two groups. It was Vernon who volunteered to not only take the second group, which was made up of those suffering the worst wounds, but he also offered to provide covering fire during the evacuation of the first group. Vernon refused to leave a man behind and assisted in safely evacuating those most seriously wounded.

As he did so, however, he found himself confronted with two machine gun posts that they'd cleverly slipped by on their way in. With the calculated toss of a hand grenade in each of the posts, Vernon ensured that the wounded men in his care were evacuated without further casualty.

Not satisfied with having killed nine German soldiers, Vernon destroyed three machine gun nests, a dugout, and an observation post. The very next night, Vernon then bravely volunteered to lead a battalion right back through the minefield and the heavy mortar fire that had inflicted such damage on his men.

Vernon led an all-white battalion safely to Castle Aghinolfi without a single American bullet being fired. Germany surrendered less than a month later, and Vernon—once a young boy who suffered a similar tragedy—had played his part in preventing any further loss for millions around the world.

The Aftermath of the Act

After the Axis forces were defeated, Vernon continued working for the Army and originally stayed in Italy as a member of the Army of Occupation. He returned home in 1947 and served as part of the 11th Airborne Division as a parachutist in the Korean War. During this time, with the racial segregation of the Army coming to an end, he was given the honor of being one of the first black commanders of an all-white company.

Vernon left the Army in 1968 after 27 years of service and then served on a tour with the American Red Cross for 20 years before retiring. Vernon married three times and had three children with his third wife. After the death of his third wife, he moved to a cabin in northern Idaho's Benewah Valley. He spent the rest of his life the way that he started it: hunting out in the wilderness, like his grandfather.

After surviving brain cancer in 2004, Vernon passed away because of the same illness in July of 2010. His family were able to attend his funeral at Arlington National Cemetery thanks to funds raised by their local community, and three other Medal of Honor recipients also attended to pay their respects.

A Lasting Legacy

Despite Vernon's legacy now being cemented into the annals of history, it once looked as though he wouldn't receive the same credit that some of his military brothers did.

Following his vital contribution in capturing Castle Aghinolfi, the soldiers who had fought alongside him nominated him for the Distinguished Service Cross (DSC). His actions, of course, merited the Medal of Honor, but with his brothers knowing that white higher-ranking soldiers would never approve a black man of such honor, they were forced to nominate him for the military's second-highest honor instead.

The DSC is undoubtedly an incredible honor for all who lay their lives on the line, but the unjustness was compounded when the captain, who claimed they were returning with reinforcements before leaving Vernon's detachment to die, was nominated for the Medal of Honor rather than Vernon.

Despite further attempts to discredit Vernon's contributions, he still received his well-deserved DSC, and I'm sure that he was incredibly proud of the commitment he'd shown to his country. He also received additional awards, including (Baker, 2021):

- Bronze Star with one oak leaf cluster and V device
- Silver Star
- Purple Heart with one oak leaf cluster

- American Campaign Medal
- American Defense Service Medal
- National Defense Service Medal with one service star
- Italian Cross of Valor of War
- Polish Cross of Valor
- European-African-Middle Eastern Campaign Medal with three Campaign stars
- Army of Occupation Medal
- Parachutist Badge
- World War II Victory Medal

At the end of World War II, Vernon was the Mediterranean Theater's most highly decorated black soldier.

The honors and accolades that Vernon received may have felt like a non-factor to the man himself. Despite feeling pride, he never considered himself a hero and was more eager to heap praise on the men he'd lost along the way (Olsen, 2010).

The United States Army took a different view. In 1993, they launched an investigation into why no black soldiers had received the Medal of Honor—an investigation which Vernon himself was skeptical of.

The Army saw their investigations through, though, and in 1997, an independent panel named Vernon as one of seven black soldiers whose actions throughout World War II were worthy of the military's highest honor.

The citation for Vernon's Medal of Honor reads:

> For conspicuous gallantry and intrepidity at the risk of his life above and beyond the call of duty: First Lieutenant Vernon J. Baker distinguished himself by extraordinary heroism in action on 5 and 6 April 1945. At 0500 hours on 5 April 1945, Lieutenant Baker advanced at the head of his weapons platoon, along with Company C's three rifle platoons, toward their objective, Castle Aghinolfi—a German mountain strong point on the high ground just east of the coastal highway and about two miles from the 370th Infantry Regiment's line of departure.
>
> Moving more rapidly than the rest of the company, Lieutenant Baker and about 25 men reached the south side of a draw some 250 yards from the castle within two hours. In reconnoitering for a suitable position to set up a machine gun, Lieutenant Baker observed two cylindrical objects pointing out a slit in a mount at the edge of a hill. Crawling up and under the opening, he stuck his M-1 into the slit and emptied the clip, killing the observation post's two occupants. Moving to another position in the same area, Lieutenant Baker stumbled upon a well-camouflaged machine gun nest, the crew of which was eating breakfast.
>
> He shot and killed both enemy soldiers. After Captain John F. Runyon, Company C's Commander joined the group, a German soldier appeared from the draw and hurled a grenade which failed to explode. Lieutenant Baker shot the enemy soldier twice as he tried to flee. Lieutenant Baker then went down into the draw alone. There he blasted open the concealed entrance of another dugout with a hand grenade, shot one German soldier who emerged after the explosion, tossed another grenade into the dugout and entered firing his sub-

> machine gun killing two more Germans. As Lieutenant Baker climbed back out of the draw, enemy machine gun and mortar fire began to inflict heavy casualties among the group of 25 soldiers, killing or wounding about two-thirds of them. When expected reinforcements did not arrive, Captain Runyon ordered a withdrawal in two groups. Lieutenant Baker volunteered to cover the withdrawal of the first group, which consisted mostly of walking wounded, and to remain to assist in the evacuation of the more seriously wounded.
>
> During the second group's withdrawal, Lieutenant Baker, supported by covering fire from one of the platoon members, destroyed two machine gun positions (previously bypassed during the assault) with hand grenades. In all, Lieutenant Baker accounted for nine enemy dead soldiers, elimination of three machine gun positions, an observation post, and a dugout. On the following night, Lieutenant Baker voluntarily led a battalion advance through enemy mine fields and heavy fire toward the division objective. Lieutenant Baker's fighting spirit and daring leadership were an inspiration to his men and exemplify the highest traditions of the military service. (Baker, 2021)

Sadly, Vernon would be the only member of the seven who was still alive to receive the honor. Following his Medal of Honor, Vernon was also invited to Italy in 1997 on the 52nd anniversary of the battle for Castle Aghinolfi. He was met by villages full of grateful Italians, who showered him with praise and honored him for the role he played in freeing their country.

Outside of his military accolades, Vernon was also awarded an honorary doctorate from Wofford College in South Carolina, as well as the Sandor Teszler Award for Moral Courage and Service to Humankind.

Three streets in Iowa were also named in his honor, too. Vernon Baker showed the importance of composure and critical thinking to earn a decisive victory despite such bloodshed.

Chapter 3:

William Soderman

United States Army, Battle of the Bulge, 1944

Through his unfaltering courage against overwhelming odds, Pfc. Soderman contributed in great measure to the defense of Rocherath, exhibiting to a superlative degree the intrepidity and heroism with which American soldiers met and smashed the savage power of the last great German offensive. – President Harry S. Truman

Background of the Hero

William was born on March 20, 1912, in West Haven, Connecticut—a town that, by the end of World War II, had seen its population cut almost in half by death. Quite simply, every family from the tight-knit communities within the city of West Haven seemed to have lost someone.

William, or Bill, would go down in the city's history as its only Medal of Honor recipient. But before becoming a hero, he was a quiet boy from Swedish immigrant parents.

His family kept to themselves and socialized mostly within their Scandinavian circle, the Swedish Apollo Society. People in West Haven took care of each other, but William was the quiet type and kept to himself more than most.

While at West Haven High School, William played football and showed athletic prowess and a will to win, and he'd need both of those qualities in abundance once the war started.

He joined the Army from his home city in August 1943, when he was 31 years old. At that time, America was deeply embroiled in World War II and needed men willing to sacrifice. In William, they found what they were looking for.

He climbed the ranks quickly and showed his proficiency with a bazooka in July of 1944 when he managed to disable a German tank with a well-placed shell on the road to France's Saint-Lô.

By December 16 of the following year, he had risen to the rank of private first class in Company K, 9th Infantry Regiment, 2nd Infantry Division.

The Heroic Act

Having been deployed in Europe when the Germans ignited the Battle of the Bulge on December 16, 1944, William was one of thousands trying to replenish his energy reserves at the Allied post within the Ardennes Forest. The Allies weren't expecting an attack, but when the Germans did so, they attacked with all the desperation and bluster of an army that knew that they were losing the war.

The Germans were calculating and picked their spot carefully, knowing that the Allies were exhausted not only from battle but also from the worst winter that northern Europe had seen in 50 years. The consistently heavy snowfall and the ice-cold temperatures were eating at the very reserves William and the Allies were trying to replenish.

Unlike the Americans, who believed the European war would be over by Christmas and subsequently allowed their military production to slow, the Germans were well prepared to fight in the freezing cold temperatures. They had ramped up their military production the month prior and produced cold-weather gear to help protect them from the cold. They also had greater experience fighting in comparable temperatures across Norway and Russia.

When the first round of German artillery struck, William was near the Belgian village of Rocherath with the mission of helping his brothers defend a key road junction. The Americans were ill-equipped, tired, and completely blindsided by the counterattack.

William saw his unit absolutely ravaged and devastated. There was simply no time to evacuate his wounded brothers, so William raised his hand to take the responsibility of handing the wounded over to the Nazis in a bid to preserve their lives. Given that the Germans had a reputation for shooting their

American prisoners in cold blood, William had already shown great heroism in suggesting such a plan. William's commanders had other concerns. They expected that rather than having an opportunity to hand any wounded over, a wave of blustering Panzer tanks would come next. They feared that the German plan was to inflict bloodshed and that they had no concern for anyone who offered to surrender.

It was do or die for William and his unit, and it was at that precise moment that he took the war into his own frozen hands. He grabbed his bazooka, multiple canvas bags packed with rockets, and supplemented his haul with a .45 Colt sidearm, M1 carbine, and as many grenades as he could carry.

Armed to the teeth, he ventured forth into the darkness alone.

The fact that William was choosing to act alone carries even more weight when you consider that bazooka operators would typically act in a two-man team with a shooter and a loader. William had previously watched his loader be brutally wounded by the artillery barrage and knew that he would have no choice but to perform both roles.

He hefted the heavy load to the woodland on the edge of a narrow road, surmising that the cover of the dark woodland might give him at least a slither of a chance of survival. His plan was to disable a lead tank and block the road for the other tanks so that his ravaged unit had enough time to withdraw to Elsenborn Ridge, which was four miles west of their location.

The plan was beyond daring, and to say that William had a slither of a chance of survival is being generous. But as the only thing standing between the Germans and the complete annihilation of his unit, he sat in wait as darkness advantageously fell around him. Losses were inevitable. In fact, the Battle of the Bulge resulted in more American casualties than any battle that had come before it (*Battle of the Bulge*, 2018).

But a total defeat was preventable if he struck at the precise moment. Deciphering when that precise moment would be was no easy task for William. He knew that as soon as he fired his bazooka, his position would illuminate the darkness that was protecting him and draw torrential fire. He also knew that he needed to be so accurate with his shot that his rocket would land in the heavily armored tank's crew compartment, igniting its ammunition rather than simply bouncing off its tough exterior.

Perhaps one of the things that he did have in his favor was the fact that the trusty bazooka that he had by his side was the latest version that American manufacturers had to offer and was capable of dealing devastating damage. The caveat was that dealing that kind of damage would require him to get dangerously close to his target.

First came the ominous rumbling of the weighty tanks, pre-empting their Nazi-insignia-emblazed hulls. Next came the fearsome sight of five Mark V Panzer tanks rounding a bend in the road a few hundred yards away.

With his bazooka loaded and his prayers repeated, William hefted the bazooka over his tired shoulder and stepped out onto the icy road defiantly in the face of the five-tank column as his American brothers sprinted for their lives in the other direction.

With the deepest breath of his life, William knelt down to steady his weapon and fired a rocket with such precision that it rattled into the crew compartment with aplomb. Before the crew that were housed in it could escape, the ammunition was ignited, and the tank erupted in a giant plume of fire that filled the night sky. The shattered tank blocked the road just as William had intended, who immediately set to working frantically in an attempt to reload despite the onslaught of fire splintering the ice around him.

The proceeding column was able to retreat before he could reload, and his position was now compromised as he'd feared. Yet, he was undeterred and retreated to the cover of the dark woodland, where he would spend the rest of the night despite the cripplingly cold temperatures.

Despite facing enemy fire and his body's desperation to shut down in the cold, William defiantly held his position and waited for the next onslaught. That second onslaught would commence under the orange glow of dawn when another five German Panzers rolled down the same narrow road, now well aware of William's position.

This time, to maintain the element of surprise, William sprinted down a ditch to meet the beasts head-on, catching them off-guard with a counterattack of his own. He sprang out into the road, once more in full view of the enemy, took a knee on the bloody and cracked ice, and sank another rocket into the heart of the lead Panzer.

He'd destroyed a second tank and halted their progress once more, raising his tank count to two. Before they could return fire, William submerged himself back within the ditch and brought his unit more crucial time to withdraw. The frustrated Germans had no option but to withdraw their second column of tanks, but William expected that they'd be back.

William was relentless in his desire to return to his unit, but with the Germans now keenly aware of his presence, he was confronted by an infantry platoon while returning to his post and utilized a combination of his sidearm and carbine to kill three and wound many others of the platoon.

When he returned to his unit, he found their position impossible to defend, and those who were fit and healthy would have to join the wounded in retreating and concede the ground they were seeking to defend.

At this point, William had more than played his part, and he could have retreated with the rest of his unit with his head held high, but the all-too-familiar rumbling of more panzers in the distance saw him shun his position of relative safety so that he could meet them head on once more to give the last of his unit the time they needed to evacuate safely.

William marched down the icy road toward the lead tank and was able to sink one last rocket into the bowels of a third and final Panzer before machine gun fire tore through his right shoulder, nearly killing him and preventing him from using the bazooka with which he'd dealt such damage to the enemy.

With no other option, he retreated to the ditch that had served him so well and dragged himself through the cold dirt to American lines, where he could be offered safe evacuation from the battlefield.

Had it not been for William's actions on December 16, 1944, the Allied body count would have been far greater.

Aftermath of the Act

William was still a private first class when he decided to leave the Army. At that point, he returned to West Haven and married Virginia Rae Leake.

They had two children, Susan and Peter.

He spent the rest of his working life at the Veterans Affairs hospital in his hometown until he died in 1980 at the age of 68.

He was laid to rest in West Haven's Oak Grove Cemetery.

A Lasting Legacy

William was honored with a Medal of Honor for his brave actions at the Battle of the Bulge. He was presented the award on the first of November in 1945; his citation reads:

> Armed with a bazooka, he defended a key road junction near Rocherath, Belgium, on 17 December 1944, during the German Ardennes counteroffensive. After a heavy artillery barrage had wounded and forced the withdrawal of his assistant, he heard enemy tanks approaching the position where he calmly waited in the gathering darkness of early evening until the five Mark V tanks which made up the hostile force were within point-blank range. He then stood up, completely disregarding the firepower that could be brought to bear upon him, and launched a rocket into the lead tank, setting it afire and forcing its crew to abandon it as the other tanks pressed on before Pfc. Soderman could reload.
>
> The daring bazooka man remained at his post all night under severe artillery, mortar, and machine-gun fire, awaiting the next onslaught, which was made shortly after dawn by five more tanks. Running along a ditch to meet them, he reached an advantageous point and there leaped to the road in full view of the tank gunners, deliberately aimed his weapon and disabled the lead tank.
>
> The other vehicles, thwarted by a deep ditch in their attempt to go around the crippled machine, withdrew. While returning to his post Pfc. Soderman, braving heavy fire to attack an enemy infantry platoon from close range, killed at least three Germans and wounded several others with a round from his bazooka. By this time, enemy pressure had made Company K's position

untenable. Orders were issued for withdrawal to an assembly area, where Pfc. Soderman was located when he once more heard enemy tanks approaching. Knowing that elements of the company had not completed their disengaging maneuver and were consequently extremely vulnerable to an armored attack, he hurried from his comparatively safe position to meet the tanks.

Once more he disabled the lead tank with a single rocket, his last; but before he could reach cover, machine-gun bullets from the tank ripped into his right shoulder. Unarmed and seriously wounded he dragged himself along a ditch to the American lines and was evacuated.

Through his unfaltering courage against overwhelming odds, Pfc. Soderman contributed in great measure to the defense of Rocherath, exhibiting to a superlative degree the intrepidity and heroism with which American soldiers met and smashed the savage power of the last great German offensive. (Soderman, 2024)

Along with his Medal of Honor, William was also awarded the following accolades (Soderman, 2024):

- Purple Heart
- European-African-Middle Eastern Campaign Medal
- American Campaign Medal
- World War II Victory Medal

In addition to his military accolades, he was also honored by the naming of two Navy ships and a cargo ship in 2002.

William Soderman and his bazooka destroyed three deadly panzer tanks to prevent the total annihilation of his unit. His bravery and precision are truly commendable.

Chapter 4:

Richard Bong

United States Air Force, the Southwest Pacific Theatre, and the Philippines Campaigns, 1941–1945

I'd go nuts if I couldn't keep on flying in combat. –Richard Bong

Background of the Hero

Richard was born on September 24, 1920. He was the first of nine children, and was raised by his Swedish father, Carl, and his American mother, Dora, on their farm in Poplar, Wisconsin.

As you would expect, growing up on a farm meant that Richard had responsibilities bestowed upon him from an early age. He was given chores across the farm, was taught how to operate and drive heavy farm machinery at an early age, and had an important role in keeping the farm running smoothly and providing food for his family.

He also engaged in fishing and hunting in the woodland and streams surrounding his family's farm, which gave him early hands-on experience with a rifle and taught him the importance of patience and attention to detail.

It was while he was working on the farm that Richard was exposed to planes for the first time, and he was very excited by what he saw! When planes carrying mail to President Coolidge's summer White House would fly overhead, Richard's imagination was captured, and a desire to one day soar through the skies was sparked. This love first manifested through plane model building, which allowed him to get hands-on with some of the flying beasts that he hoped to fly one day.

Richard was a stereotypical, ideal American boy. Despite possessing a daring cheekiness, he was raised with important core values by his family. He had great manners and was respectful to those around him. He simply loved his family and the country that had welcomed his father in with open arms.

Richard enrolled at Poplar High School in 1934, where he was a keen and talented athlete. The physical toll of growing up on a farm had served him well, and he excelled in hockey, basketball, and baseball. While his physical fitness was an asset, he was also very much in touch with the arts. He played clarinet in the marching band as well as singing in the choir.

Richard was a doer who had his hand in many pies. He wanted to participate and contribute and was never happy sitting still. He needed to fly—metaphorically as well as literally!

One of his school projects saw him combine academia with his roots when he planted a tree on the family farm to help his father. With good grades and a great attitude, Richard excelled throughout the three years he spent at Poplar before he transferred to Central High School in Superior for his senior year.

Richard graduated from Central in 1938 without any hiccups and was then free to pursue his true passion—flying.

The next step in his educational journey took him to Superior State Teachers College in the same year, where he enrolled in the Civilian Pilot Training Program and would have his first taste of taking to the skies. He did so like a duck to water and soon convinced his family to help him supplement his education with private flying lessons.

On May 29, 1941, Richard took the brave step of enlisting in the Army Corps Aviation Cadet Program, where one of his flight instructors was future U.S. Senator Barry Goldwater.

While his instructors could see that Richard was a natural, they, of course, had no idea of the stunning feats he would later achieve behind the controls of a fighter plane.

However, before Richard could achieve those feats, he had to graduate, which he did in January 1942. Upon graduation, Richard achieved the rank of second lieutenant and was assigned as a gunnery instructor in Arizona.

Given that America had officially joined World War II just a month prior, Richard knew he would soon be taking to the skies to fight for the two most important things to him: his family and his country.

Richard's first operational assignment came on May 6, when he was sent to Hamilton Field in California to join the 49th Fighter Squadron (FS), 14th Fighter Group. During this time, he was taught how to fly the twin-engine Lockheed P-38 Lightning.

Before Richard's heroics, the cheekiness that had presented itself during his childhood would resurface, and he soon found himself facing disciplinary action.

On the 12th of June, in a unique form of celebration, Richard buzzed over the house of a pilot who had recently married and was promptly grounded and cited for breaking flying rules. It was also found that Richard had joined a trio of pilots looping around the Golden Gate Bridge and had even blown the clothes off a clothesline.

He was breaking the rules and being far from a model soldier; however, he was also showing something else that his country needed at that time—guts and the willingness to throw caution to the wind.

When General George C. Kenney personally reprimanded Richard, he admitted as such when he told him that his desire to perform craziness in his plane made him an asset to the Air Force. When writing the disciplinary measures up, Kenney added that the Air Force "needed" kids like Richard (Kenney, 1949, pp. 3–6).

Richard may have been showing ill-discipline, but in doing so, he was showing the balls that would be needed to take to the skies in combat.

Despite denying much of the wrongdoing that was leveled at him, Richard was still grounded when his group flew to England in July. After serving his disciplinary period, Richard was sent to the Southwest Pacific as part of the 84th Fighter Squadron of the 78th Fighter Group.

Around this time, Richard saw himself bounce between fighter units and was eventually assessed as skillful enough to transfer his skills flying the P-40 Warhawk and P-39 Airacobra to the P-38 Lightning, a plane he would eventually become synonymous with.

The Heroic Act

Richard's heroism isn't confined to one specific, grandiose act of valor. His heroic acts took place throughout the Second World War II, and he eventually became recognized as the greatest pilot that the Air Force had ever seen.

While most of Richard's incredible feats would take place at the controls of his trusty P-38 Lightning, it was actually while he was awaiting its delivery that he claimed his first aerial victory.

While flying missions and gaining combat experience in New Guinea, Richard shot both a *Nakajima Ki-43 Oscar* and a *Mitsubishi A6M Zero* down during the Battle of Buna-Gona. What made this victory even more impressive was the method that Richard employed and would continue to employ throughout the war. Fearing he couldn't trust his shooting skills, Richard got in as close as possible so that he simply couldn't miss his target.

His willingness to throw caution to the wind would, of course, also put him in grave danger, and at times, he would even fly right through the debris of downed targets to surprise the next one.

Richard's actions over the village of Buna would see him awarded the Silver Star, but he was far from done. Finally equipped with his beloved P-38, Richard rejoined the 9th FS in January 1943. Stationed at Schwimmer Field near Port Moresby, he was quickly promoted to first lieutenant and would soon take to the skies over the city of Lae to annihilate not one but four more Japanese fighters.

It was during this time that Richard cemented his daring approach to battle, torpedoing through smoke and debris and even using the plane itself to smash into the enemy. His success wasn't going unnoticed, and he was soon awarded the Distinguished Service Cross for his actions over Lae before being promoted to captain.

Richard was reassigned as an assistant operations officer in November 1943 and tasked with overseeing the manufacturing of replacement airplanes. Throughout this period, he continued flying combat missions and racked up a further 19 plane kills, bringing his total count up to an incredible 25.

At this time, the Americans were rotating their best pilots to keep them fresh and allow them to train the next crop to ensure there wasn't a drop in standards. Richard was rotated out and allowed to return to the United States on leave. It was while he was there that he met Majorie Vattendahl at a college homecoming event and the pair began dating.

When Richard returned to the Southwest Pacific in January 1944, he renamed his P-38 after his beloved *Marge* and stuck a photo of her on its nose to remind him of who was waiting back home for him once he'd fulfilled the mission.

In March of the same year, another pilot was flying *Marge* when it suffered engine failure, and he was forced to bail out. The plane crashed in New Guinea and the pilot survived, but Richard was in need of another plane.

He would soon become very comfortable in his replacement P-38 and shoot down his 26th and 27th Japanese planes in a feat that saw him surpass a record that was set during World War I by pilot Eddie Rickenbacker. Eddie had destroyed 26 planes for the Americans, and now Richard was in a class all of his own (*Richard Bong*, 2023).

Shortly after, General Kenney promoted him to the rank of major and sent him home to train other pilots in Texas. The bulk of Richard's work was seemingly done, and he was tasked with visiting training bases to advise other pilots before being sent on a 15-state bond promotional tour.

When Richard returned to New Guinea in September of 1944, he was assigned as an advanced gunnery instructor. While he was still given permission to embark on missions, he was also ordered not to seek combat.

Whether Richard sought combat or not, it found him.

On voluntary missions throughout the Philippines campaign, he flew 30 more combat missions and implemented his brash and up-and-coming style of combat to destroy another 12 planes.

By the end of World War II, Richard Bong had destroyed an astounding 40 enemy planes alone (*Richard Bong*, 2023). It is therefore far from hyperbole to suggest that Richard contributed significantly to the Allies' eventual victory.

The Aftermath of the Act

Richard was recommended for the Medal of Honor in 1944 and would be sent home for good in January 1945. He married Marjorie in February of 1945 and continued to attend war bond tours and make public appearances.

Richard and planes were inseparable. He became a test pilot and was assigned to Lockheed's plant in California. Tasked with testing the P-80 Shooting Star jet fighter, he was sadly killed on August 6, 1945, when the fuel pump malfunctioned.

It's believed that Richard didn't eject from the plane early enough to save his own life because he stayed at the controls to steer the plane away from the houses of civilians. His death occurred on the same day that the Americans dealt the decisive blow of dropping the atomic bomb on Hiroshima.

Richard's status was such that his funeral was attended by thousands of people who wanted to pay their respects, and the streets were lined by hundreds more across his funeral route. He was laid to rest in Wisconsin's Poplar cemetery in his family's plot.

Having ensured the freedom of his country, he was reunited with his beloved family.

A Lasting Legacy

Richard was awarded the Medal of Honor in December 1944 by General Douglas MacArthur. His citation reads:

> For conspicuous gallantry and intrepidity in action above and beyond the call of duty in the Southwest Pacific area from October 10 to November 15, 1944. Though assigned to duty as gunnery instructor and neither required nor expected to perform combat duty, Maj. Bong voluntarily and at his own urgent request engaged in repeated combat missions, including unusually hazardous sorties over Balikpapan, Borneo, and in the Leyte area of the Philippines.

> His aggressiveness and daring resulted in his shooting down 8 enemy airplanes during this period. (Medal of Honor Recipients - World War II (A-F), 2008)

Alongside his Medal of Honor, Richard was also awarded the following (*Richard Bong Ace of Aces*, n.d.):

- United States Army Air Forces pilot badge
- Distinguished Service Cross
- Air Medal with one Bronze Oak Leaf Cluster
- Air Medal with two Bronze Oak Leaf Clusters and two Silver Oak Leaf Clusters
- Silver Star with one Bronze Oak Leaf Cluster
- Distinguished Flying Cross with one Bronze Oak Leaf Cluster and one Silver Oak Leaf Cluster
- American Defense Service Medal
- American Campaign Medal
- Philippine Liberation Medal with one 3/16" Bronze Star
- Asiatic-Pacific Campaign Medal with one 3/16" Silver Star
- World War II Victory Medal

Alongside Richard's deserved military honors, his legacy was further consolidated in the mid-1950s when his name was planned to be used for the construction of a new USAF installation.

After complications during the construction, it was eventually abandoned. However, the former base site is today called the *Richard Bong State Recreation Area.*

Ten years after Richard's death, a memorial was erected in his hometown for him. Funds were then subsequently raised for the development of the Richard I Bong Veterans Historical Center in his hometown, too. The center contains a screening room, a museum, and a restored plane that resembles Richard's beloved *Marge.*

On Route 2 in the United States, between Duluth, Minnesota, and Superior, Wisconsin, sits a bridge named in Richard's honor, and there is also a bridge in Australia of the same name.

In Richard's hometown of Poplar, there is also an airport named in his honor.

The Aviation Challenge Program contains barracks named after Richard, and there is also a squadron at the Arnold Air Society at the University of Wisconsin named after him.

Japan is home to the Richard Bong Theatre and *Bong Avenues,* which are also located in San Antonio, Arizona, Alaska, and Louisiana.

Bong Terrace is a neighborhood that was built between 1956 and 1957, and *Bong Street* leads to the National Museum of the United States Air Force.

As if that wasn't enough, Richard was inducted into the National Aviation Hall of Fame in 1986 and the Wisconsin Aviation Hall of Fame a year later. In 2003, the United States Air Force Academy named Richard as their class exemplar, and in 2018, he was also inducted into the International Air and Space Hall of Fame.

In 2024, after years of searching, the wreckage of Richard's beloved plane, *Marge,* was found in the jungles of New Guinea. What remains of the incredible symbol of bravery and sacrifice can now be seen in the Papua New Guinea museum, serving as a reminder of the importance of freedom.

Richard Bong was such a truly incredible fighter pilot that he could lay claim to being the greatest that America has ever seen.

Chapter 5:

Ruby Bradley

United States Army Nurse Corps, Santo Tomas Internment Camp, 1943–1945

It was all in a day's work. –Ruby Bradley

The Background of the Hero

Ruby Bradley was born on December 19, 1907, and was born and raised on a family farm in Spencer, West Virginia.

In 1926, at the age of 19, Ruby took her first steps into a teaching career when she graduated from Glenville State Teachers College. She went on to teach for four years in Roane County's crowded one-room schoolhouses, where she taught all eight grades within a single classroom.

While teaching in Roane County, she showed great empathy for the students who were going hungry due to the Great Depression. She showed so much empathy, in fact, that Ruby began bringing food into school to feed those hit the hardest by the economic climate.

Ruby felt that she could be doing more to help those in need. So, she made the decision to spend a day with her sister on the wards of the hospital where she worked in Washington, D.C.

While Ruby was there, she fell in love with the possibility of helping so many patients and alleviating their suffering. Her mind was quickly made up, and in 1930, she enrolled in the Philadelphia General Hospital School of Nursing with the goal of becoming a top-flight surgical nurse.

She was fiercely committed to her goal, and would spend every day between the hours of 7 a.m. and midnight either studying diligently or learning her trade on the wards of the hospital.

She graduated in 1933 after three hard years of study, and very quickly became a favorite of both the patients that she was treating and the surgeons that she was tasked with assisting. She was good-natured and gentle with everyone around her, which, combined with her easy smile and undoubtable skill, made her a very valuable asset to the hospital.

It would then be her sense of adventure, paired with her desire to continue working with her sister, which led her to join the Walter Reed Army Medical Center in 1934 as a surgical nurse.

The Center posed a new challenge for Ruby, with most of its 1,225 beds typically filled. Despite the added pressure that came with the role, Ruby continued to excel and impress her peers and patients at the Center.

In January of 1940, Ruby was transferred from Washington to Manila in the Philippines, where she was assigned to a hospital on the Island of Corregidor in the bay. True to form, she was soon very popular amongst fellow professionals and her patients, and she set the bar high, regularly working through the night.

She would transfer again in early 1941 when she was reassigned to Camp John Hay on the island of Luzon. There, she worked as a surgical nurse and chief nurse until her world was turned upside down on December 7 that year when the Japanese struck Pearl Harbor.

The Heroic Act

First, Ruby was faced with bombs dropped by the strafing Japanese that forced her to hide in shelters with other staff and patients. Then, once things had started to ease somewhat, she had the small matter of wounded soldiers and civilians flooding through the hospital doors.

Little did Ruby know that things were about to become much more dangerous. After they had bombed Camp John Hay, the Japanese swarmed the hospital and wrestled control of the camp from the fast-evacuating Americans. On the day of their invasion on December 23, the hospital had been so stretched and inundated with the wounded that Ruby had personally assisted in 37 separate operations. The Americans at Camp John Hay were vulnerable and clinging to the ropes, and the Japanese knew it. With little chance of survival, Ruby frantically helped round up whatever supplies they could get their hands on and helped load patients into wagons to escape via the surrounding hills.

Sadly, their evacuation plans were soon blocked by approaching Japanese troops, and many of the patients that Ruby was trying to help save would find themselves dragged back to the American-military-base-turned-Japanese-prison camp.

Ruby initially managed to evade capture when she fled to the hills with two of her colleagues and found refuge in a logging camp where they cared for civilian refugees. However, after five days, they found themselves betrayed by a couple from the logging camp and were forced to surrender to Japanese soldiers.

Ruby found herself back in the military base that she'd called home, only now she was there as a prisoner of war. The occupants were cramped into a building that contained 500 people, and the situation looked beyond dire.

Incredibly, though, Ruby refused to let her spirit fade and instead saw her desire to help those around burn brighter than ever. Despite the chilling warning that one escapee would result in the death of five others, she cheekily began smuggling equipment and drugs into their building via the camp hospital so that she could set up a dispensary within the prison camp.

Equipped with morphine used in the First World War and equipment that was far from fit for purpose, Ruby amazingly managed to perform an appendectomy on just her third day in the camp. The Japanese watched in disbelief as she was able to perform such a feat without the right tools. She was creative and even managed to combine a tea strainer and gauze to anesthetize a woman with ether when she went into labor. She had always wanted to help those around her, and now those around her needed her help more than ever. But her fellow prisoners were benefiting from more than just her physical skills; they also needed her resilience and spirit.

When they ran out of soap, she encouraged her fellow prisoners to make their own by mixing fats with lye from wood ashes. When they were forced to eat worms, she did so for the good of her country and joked with those around her about the protein content!

After spending 37 months at the former American military base, Ruby was transferred to the Santo Tomas Internment Camp in Manila in 1943. At the time of her transfer, she had assisted in the delivery of 13 babies and played a key role in 230 major operations (Bradley, 2019).

She perhaps hadn't realized at the time, but this transfer was going to see Ruby tested more than she had ever been. The conditions at the Santo Tomas camp were far worse than those at Camp Hay, and despite her best efforts, patients would die on a daily basis.

She diligently helped where she could, selflessly saving the half cup portions of rice that she would receive in the morning and evening so that she could share hers with the young children when they started to cry out of hunger. Just as Ruby had once done as a teacher, she was once again feeding starving children.

Of course, Ruby must have been starving, too, but rather than worry about her own needs, she started stealing extra food so that she could provide more for the children, undeterred by the risk of severe punishment or her own crippling starvation.

Her selflessness, along with that of the other imprisoned nurses, saw the other prisoners bestow the nickname of "Angels in Fatigues" upon them (McLellan, 2002).

It should come as no surprise that by the time the Santo Tomas Internment Camp was liberated on February 3, 1945, she had shrunk down to 84 pounds. She was tired, hungry, and scarred—but she was alive.

Aftermath of the Act

Following her liberation, Ruby returned home to West Virginia for a period of recovery. No one would have begrudged her the opportunity to start fresh with a new career as far from the battlefield as possible at that point, and she had more than served her country.

As I'm sure you've gathered by now, however, Ruby was made of much sterner stuff than the average person.

Five years following her liberation, she put her life back on the line for her country during the Korean War and served as the Chief Nurse of the 171st Evacuation Hospital. Her devotion and bravery would later lead her to be promoted to Chief Nurse for the Eighth Army in 1951, which gave her the responsibility of overseeing 500 Army nurses across Korea.

The role would see her come within seconds of losing her life when a Chinese counter-offensive led to 100,000 Chinese Communist troops ambushing the American troops that she was frantically working to patch up (Bradley, 2019).

With the troops just five miles up the road from her position and closing fast, Ruby refused to board the plane that had been sent to evacuate her and the soldiers in her care until her last patient was safely on the plane. Her selflessness saw her only evade an enemy shell that blew her ambulance up by mere seconds. Even in the face of grave danger, Ruby was putting the needs of others before her own.

After the Korean War, Ruby returned home and lived a full life, working as a civilian nurse in Roane County and purchasing a ranch near her family. She lived until the age of 94 when she died of natural causes and was buried in Arlington National Cemetery.

A Lasting Legacy

Upon her return home from Korea in 1953, Ruby became the first woman to receive a guard salute when she received a full-dress honor guard ceremony. Her hometown also honored her with a parade (McLellan, 2002).

She continued to serve in the Army and became just the third woman in the history of the Army to reach the rank of colonel in 1958. She would finally conclude her service to her country in 1963 when she retired from active duty (McLellan, 2002).

She did so as the most decorated woman in the history of the U.S. Army, and her decorations, medals, and ribbons included (Norman, 2013, p. 317):

- American Campaign Medal
- American Defense Service Medal with a "Foreign Service" clasp
- Army Commendation Medal with an oak leaf cluster
- Army of Occupation Medal with a "Japan" clasp
- Asiatic-Pacific Campaign Medal with two campaign stars
- Bronze Star Medal with an oak leaf cluster

- Florence Nightingale Medal (International Red Cross)
- Korean Service Medal with three campaign stars
- Korean War Service Medal (Republic of Korea)
- Legion of Merit with an oak leaf cluster
- Meritorious Unit Commendation
- National Defense Service Medal with a star
- Philippine Defense Medal (Republic of Philippines) with a star
- Philippine Independence Medal (Republic of Philippines)
- Philippine Liberation Medal (Republic of Philippines) with a star
- Presidential Unit Citation with an oak leaf cluster
- Prisoner of War Medal
- United Nations Service Medal
- World War II Victory Medal

When you include Ruby's additional citations and awards, the total count of honors she received reaches an incredible 34.

In 1954, she was featured and honored on the television show *This is Your Life,* and her hometown celebrated *Ruby Bradley Day* in 2007 on what would have been her centenary birthday.

Unlike many of the heroes that we've read about so far, Ruby has made her feelings explicitly clear when she was asked how she would like to be remembered:

"As just an Army nurse" (Smith, 2023).

I think we can all respectfully agree that Ruby Bradley went far beyond the duty of an Army nurse and is much more deserving of being known as an American hero, too.

Chapter 6:

Ernest E. Evans

United States Navy, Battle off Samar, 1944

This is going to be a fighting ship. I intend to go in harm's way, and anyone who doesn't want to go along had better get off right now. –Ernest E. Evans

Background of the Hero

Ernest Evans was born on August 13, 1908. Ernest was of Native American ancestry and was born in Pawnee, Oklahoma.

After graduating from Muskogee's Central High School, he enlisted in the U.S. Navy in 1926. He was appointed to the U.S. Naval Academy in Maryland after a year of training, at which point he was bestowed the rank of midshipman.

After four years at the academy, Ernest graduated with a Bachelor of Science degree and the rank of commissioned ensign. However, just a year later, he was promoted to the rank of commander.

Ernest was on his way up, being assigned to the Naval Air Station in San Diego, California, in 1931. After a year at the station, he was on the move again, serving across the *USS Colorado, Roper, and Rathburne* in consecutive stints.

Next, he found himself stationed in Pensacola, Florida, at their Naval Air Station, where he boarded the *USS Pensacola.* After serving on the *Pensacola* for six months, he continued his steady rise and was promoted further, becoming an aviation gunnery observer as part of the ship's Scouting Squadron NINE.

He spent the next four years at sea serving on the *USS Chaumont, Cahokia, and Black Hawk* consecutively and established himself as a trusted and brave servant of his country.

It was in August of 1941 that Ernest was given an assignment that would change his life: joining the crew on the USS Destroyer *Aiden.* Ernest was serving on *Aiden* in the Pacific Ocean at the time of the attack on Pearl Harbor. Just three months after the attack, Ernest was presented with the greatest opportunity and promotion of his stellar career to date:

He assumed command of the *Aiden* on March 14, 1942, a role which he then fulfilled until July of the next year. While under his command, the *Aiden* served in successful operations throughout Australia, Dutch East Indies, and New Guinea.

Ernest had been so successful and led with such distinction that on October 27, 1943, he was chosen to lead a new destroyer, the *USS Johnston,* which was the ship that would eventually become intertwined with Ernest's heroic actions.

The Heroic Act

Ernest's first job was taking charge of the *Johnston's* fitting at Washington's Seattle-Tacoma Shipbuilding Corporation. The ship was commissioned on October 27, 1943, at which point he assumed command.

He first shipped out of the Pacific to participate in the Marshall Islands campaign. Under Ernest's command, the *Johnston* bombarded Kwajalein's beaches and provided vital anti-submarine support in the Caroline Islands.

Ernest and his crew were having a major impact on the war, collaborating with U.S. destroyers *Haggard* and *Franks* to sink the Japanese submarine 1-176. Ernest skillfully maneuvered the *Johnston* into position to make audible contact with the beast below before dropping heavy depth charges that resulted in an implosion below the surface and oil and debris rushing to the surface.

The destruction of the submarine ensured the safety of the immediate naval fleet, and Ernest's role in sinking it would later earn him a Bronze Star with a Combat "V." He then led his crew through Guam to provide protection and support for escort carriers, all while the *Johnston* bombarded enemy targets to such effect that the US was able to liberate the Philippine

Islands. At this point the *Johnston* joined the naval task unit Taffy 3, with the Battle of Leyte Gulf on the horizon. Taffy 3 consisted of three destroyers, four destroyer escorts, and six escort carriers. It was on October 25, 1944, that Taffy 3 made its move. Supported aerially by planes from Taffy 2, they engaged Japanese defenses far superior to them in armor, firepower, and number.

Ernest's role at the helm of the *Johnston* was to form a key part of escorting aircraft carriers that had suffered heavy damage at the hands of the Japanese fleet after traveling through the night.

Ernest positioned himself and his men right in the line of fire upon first sighting the Japanese fleet. His previous words and the promise of the *Johnston* being a fighting ship must have been ringing in the ears of his men in tandem with Japanese gunfire as the *Johnston* thrust forward without hesitation and secreted a smoke screen for the escort carriers in their party.

Seeing the inevitability of the overwhelming Japanese force that was converging upon them and fearing that their escort mission would fail, Ernest ordered that the *Johnston* break rank, parting away from Taffy 3's circular antiaircraft disposition and instead hurtling through the waves toward the approaching enemy.

Ernest left the relatively safety of the numbers he had been afforded and accelerated the ship he had been entrusted with directly toward the overwhelming enemy.

As you would expect in such a situation, Ernest's chances of success were razor-thin, and death looked almost certain. Facts that weren't lost on him and only added to the sheer heroism of his actions. Ernest told his men via the ship's intercom that a large Japanese fleet was headed for them, and that despite the overwhelming numbers that they were facing, and their slim chance of survival, they were going to "do what damage we can" (*Ernest E. Evans*, 2024). The *Johnston* caught the approaching Japanese fleet off-guard, first attacking their heavy cruiser, *Kumano,* with a volley of 5-inch shells before Ernest ordered them to launch their torpedo battery. When they did so, they did to truly devastating effect.

Three torpedoes struck the bow of the *Kumano* and ripped it clean off, forcing the immediate withdrawal of the damaged ship, alongside the heavy cruiser *Suzuya* as an escort. By default, Ernest had overseen the removal of two key Japanese pieces from the choppy waters of the chess board.

There was no time for Ernest and his men to celebrate, however, as they were immediately blasted by a barrage of Japanese shells that caused huge damage to Ernest and his crew, as well as rupturing the ship's bridge.

Despite having two fingers blown off and his shirt torn from his body, Ernest refused painkillers and ordered that the medical attention and supplies were instead afforded to his crew.

Undeterred by the severe damage they were carrying, Ernest refused to retreat and ordered his crippled ship onwards. They fought valiantly against the battleship *Haruna* and the heavy cruiser *Haguro.*

Having lost their engine power and means of communication, Ernest raced back and forth to scream steering orders down an open hatch to those turning the rudder by hand. All the while, he was still able to keep the *Johnston* in a position between the Japanese ships and the American carriers he was tasked with escorting.

When Ernest realized that the American escort carrier, *Gambier Bay*, was under fire and in dire need of support, he moved quickly to do so and turned his attention to the heavy cruiser, *Chikuma.*

However, they were intercepted by a destroyer line that bombarded the *Johnston* with such ferocity that it disabled the ship and left it without functioning weaponry.

With the *Johnston* taking on water by the second, Ernest and his crew must have feared one last devastating blow as the Japanese destroyer, *Yukikaze*, moved ominously toward them to point-blank range.

Rather than shoot, however, the destroyer saluted Ernest and his men's efforts in an act of respect.

After three exhausting hours of battle, the *Johnston* sank at 10:11 a.m. While the true fate of Ernest was never concluded, with some claiming he was killed in shellfire and others believing he escaped via a damaged motorboat, what is known is that he lived long enough to order his crew to abandon ship and that his body was never recovered.

Ernest acted with such aggression and bravery that the Japanese fleet that eventually downed him was forced to retreat out of fear that they were facing a much larger force, aborting their mission to attack the landing beaches at Leyte.

His bravery may have cost him his life, but it also saved countless others who would have been vulnerable to the Japanese fleet on the aforementioned landing beaches had they not been deterred by the efforts of Ernest and his men.

Aftermath of the Act

Ernest died at the age of 36, but he did so as a hero, ensuring that his crew abandoned ship before he was never seen again. His name is proudly emblazoned on the "Walls of the Missing" in Manila's American Cemetery.

A Lasting Legacy

Ernest was awarded the Medal of Honor posthumously on September 28, 1945. His citation reads:

> For conspicuous gallantry and intrepidity at the risk of his life above and beyond the call of duty as commanding officer of the U.S.S. Johnston in action against major units of the enemy Japanese fleet during the battle off Samar on 25 October 1944. The first to lay a smokescreen and to open fire as an enemy task force, vastly superior in number, firepower and armor, rapidly approached. Comdr. Evans gallantly diverted the powerful blasts of hostile guns from the lightly armed and armored carriers under his protection, launching the first torpedo attack when the Johnston came under straddling Japanese shellfire.
>
> Undaunted by damage sustained under the terrific volume of fire, he unhesitatingly joined others of his group to provide fire support during subsequent torpedo attacks against the Japanese and, outshooting and outmaneuvering the enemy as he consistently interposed his vessel between the hostile fleet units and our carriers despite the crippling loss of engine power and communications with steering aft, shifted command to the fantail, shouted steering orders through an open hatch to men turning the rudder by hand and battled furiously until the Johnston, burning and shuddering from a mortal blow, lay dead in the water after 3 hours of fierce combat.
>
> Seriously wounded early in the engagement, Comdr. Evans, by his indomitable courage and brilliant professional skill, aided materially in turning back the enemy during a critical phase of the action.

> His valiant fighting spirit throughout this historic battle will venture as an inspiration to all who served with him. (Evans, 2024)

His Medal of Honor was supplemented by the following military awards (*SECNAV Names Ship after World War II Hero, Medal of Honor Recipient Ernest E. Evans*, 2023):

- Bronze Star Medal with a Combat "V"
- Purple Heart
- President Unit Citation
- China Service Medal
- American Defense Service Medal with Fleet Clasp (3/16" Bronze Star)
- American Campaign Medal
- Asiatic-Pacific Campaign Medal with a 3/16" Bronze Star, and 3/16" Silver Star
- Philippine Liberation Medal with a 3/16" Bronze Star
- World War II Victory Medal

Along with Ernest's official military awards, he was honored in 1955 when a destroyer escort was named in his honor. In 2013, Rhode Island's Naval Station in Newport dedicated a virtual simulator for ship handling training after him, too, by naming it the *Evans Full Mission-2 Simulator* in Evans' honor.

After a campaign was started in 2013 to name another ship after Ernest, it was announced 10 years later that an Arleigh Burke-class destroyer would carry his name.

Ernest Evans showed such bravery that he was saluted by the enemy who had taken his life, and his actions ensured the safe transportation of six escort carriers. He served the US Navy with distinction and should never be forgotten.

Chapter 7:

John Finn

United States Navy, Pearl Harbor, 1941

That damned hero stuff is a bunch of crap, I guess. You gotta understand that there's all kinds of heroes, but they never got a chance to be in a hero's position. –John Finn

Background of the Hero

John Finn was born in Compton, California, on July 24, 1909.

As a child, he struggled to focus and sit still, which led to him dropping out of school after just the seventh grade. Struggling for somewhere to land, John spent his teenage years working odd jobs and seeking a clear path, which he eventually found in 1926, just shy of his 17th birthday.

John enlisted in the Navy in July 1926 and was quick to complete his recruit training in San Diego's Marine Corps Depot. John was surrounded by those brave enough to fight for their country, but there weren't many who would prove themselves to be as brave as him.

After a brief stint with a ceremonial guard company, he traveled to Illinois, where he attended the Naval Station in Great Lakes and enrolled in General Aviation Utilities Training.

After graduating in December, by April, he had already returned to San Diego, where he took up a post at the Naval Air Station in North Island. John worked his way up from repairing aircrafts to working as an aviation ordnanceman, and then eventually being entrusted to work on the anti-aircraft guns, which he would later become synonymous with.

John's wish to travel and see the world was realized when he was stationed on a series of ships that took him the length and breadth of the country. He served on the *USS Houston*, the *USS Lexington*, *USS Saratoga*, *USS Cincinnati*, and the *USS Jason*.

John wasn't merely enjoying the sights, though—far from it. He was grafting and working his way up the ranks at a speed many simply couldn't achieve. After nine short years of active duty, he had been promoted all the way up to the highest enlisted Navy rank of the time period—Chief Petty Officer.

Despite being lauded by those around him, John's achievements were downplayed by the man himself. John conceded that he was regarded as "Boy Wonder," but humbly claimed his achievements were more down to the "right place, right time" paradox (*John William Finn*, 2023).

The Heroic Act

One thing is for certain: On the morning of December 7, 1941, John was in the right place at the right time to save countless lives.

By 1941, he was stationed at Hawaii's Naval Air Station Kaneohe Bay and had risen even higher, reaching the rank of Chief Aviation Ordnanceman and being tasked with leading 20 men in maintaining the weapons of PBY Naval patrol planes.

Living just a mile from the base and sleeping soundly with his wife beside him, John was awoken by a popping noise just before 8 a.m. that would change his life and the lives of thousands of his comrades.

The popping, which he initially dismissed as inconsiderate idiots at gunnery practice at such an early hour, was quickly followed by the thundering of a frantic fist at his front door. John sprang from his bed and was met by the pale face of one of his men's wives when he opened the front door.

He sought answers, but all she could muster was a finger to the planes soaring above before she scarpered in fear. Still unaware of the cause of the commotion and oblivious of the origin of the planes, John left his wife in the safety of their marital home and rushed to his car. John was a man who did things by the book, so much so, in fact, that he stuck to the strict 20-mile-per-hour speed limit of the hanger base as he approached the commotion.

The sight of a Japanese bomber overhead, however, forced John to finally slam his pedal to the metal, realizing that they were under attack. John raced to the hangar where he was proudly stationed, passing row after row of the PBY planes that he was tasked with maintaining, each now a raging inferno. When he reached his destination, he found the hanger engulfed in flames, too.

He slid his car to a screeching halt and had mere seconds to take in the harrowing scene. Many of his men were fighting fires within the grounded PBY planes so that they could get behind the controls of their weaponry to return fire. Others were firing back within planes as they burned. Meanwhile, other desperate soldiers dragged the machine guns out of the planes and hulked them onto makeshift mounts made from pieces of pipe to the same effect.

The hangar and the men that worked within it were falling around John. Given that he was still in the comparative sanctity of his car, it's fair to say that he still had the means to flee what was a desperate and impossible fight.

Despite the desperation and impossibility facing him, "fight" was exactly what John chose to do that day. Leaving his means of escape behind, John dragged a .50 caliber machine gun from one of the burning PBY planes, fixing it to a mobile gun mount and positioning himself in such a manner that he had the clearest sight of the enemy—which, of course, gave them clear sight of him, too.

Despite having very little chance of hitting the Japanese fighters rushing overhead, John valiantly and defiantly spent two hours laying down fire against the ruthless enemy. With shrapnel incapacitating his left arm, a bullet having passed through one of his feet, and being soaked in blood from 21 individual wounds that littered his body like a bloody mosaic, John remained stubbornly, defiantly at his post.

All the while, he volleyed rounds back at the planes until the last one had disappeared over the horizon. Once the dust had settled and the attack was over, John disobeyed orders to seek the medical attention he desperately needed, instead choosing to help his men frantically rearm and repair their decimated fleet.

His wounds were so severe that once he was finally convinced to attend the hospital, he was kept there for more than two weeks.

Incredibly, the man himself did his best to downplay the role that he played that day, calling his 21 wounds "nothing" and assuring his amazed admirers that he never "shot down anything" (*John William Finn*, 2012).

Whether John did indeed shoot down or even hit anything is inconsequential. He stood and fought in a battle with impossible odds at a time when he had the opportunity to turn and flee. I'm sure we can all agree that he's an American hero who should be recognized and remembered.

The Aftermath of the Act

In the five years that followed, John served as a Limited Duty Officer, having received yet another promotion before eventually being promoted once more to a lieutenant of the Bombing Squadron VB-102 aboard the USS Hancock. In September 1956, John retired from the Navy as a lieutenant.

After his retirement, John lived on a 90-acre ranch in California with his wife, where they fostered and raised five Native-American children. This selfless act saw them embraced by the Campo Band of Diegueno Mission Indians. Throughout his retirement, John made frequent appearances at events held to honor veterans, including a National Medal of Honor Day ceremony in 2009 that saw him brush shoulders with former President Barack Obama. Undeterred by his walking sticks, John witnessed the laying of a wreath at the Tomb of the Unknown Soldier before attending the White House as an honorary guest of the President.

On his 100th birthday, a crowd of more than 2,000 people celebrated his achievements. He was even presented with an American flag by the Association of Aviation Ordnancemen that had been flown by each of the 11 active aircraft carriers in service at the time.

John lived with his wife Alice until she passed away in 1998, and he would live until May 27, 2010, when he passed away at the Chula Vista Veterans Home at the age of 100 years old.

He was fittingly buried right beside his beloved wife in the Campo Indian Reservation cemetery.

A Lasting Legacy

John was deservedly honored with a Medal of Honor, which would be the first one awarded for their efforts through World War II. John's was awarded in 1942 by Admiral Chester Nimitz while aboard the *USS Enterprise,* and his doting wife Alice was in attendance. His citation reads:

> For extraordinary heroism, distinguished service, and devotion above and beyond the call of duty. During the first attack by Japanese airplanes on the Naval Air Station, Kaneohe Bay, Territory of Hawaii, on December 7, 1941, he promptly secured and manned a .50 caliber machine gun mounted on an instruction stand in a completely exposed section of the parking ramp, which was under heavy enemy machine gun strafing fire.

> Although painfully wounded many times, he continued to man this gun and to return the enemy's fire vigorously and with telling effect throughout the enemy strafing and bombing attacks and with complete disregard for his own personal safety. It was only by specific orders that he was persuaded to leave his post to seek medical attention.
>
> Following first-aid treatment, although obviously suffering much pain and moving with great difficulty, he returned to the squadron area and actively supervised the rearming of returning planes. His extraordinary heroism and conduct in this action are considered to be in keeping with the highest traditions of the Naval Service. (Lieutenant John William Finn, USN, (1909-2010), 2012)

As the last surviving Medal of Honor recipient from the attack on Pearl Harbor, John also held the honor of being the oldest living recipient of the award. He is also the only aviation ordnanceman to receive the Medal of Honor to this day.

Supplementing his Medal of Honor were the following awards (*John William Finn*, 2010):

- Purple Heart
- Good Conduct Medal with two service stars
- American Campaign Medal
- Navy Unit Commendation
- American Defense Service Medal
- World War II Victory Medal

- Yangtze Service Medal
- Asiatic-Pacific Campaign Medal with five battle stars

John was further honored when a Marine Corps base in Hawaii renamed one of its headquarters buildings in his honor, as well as a boat used to ferry visitors to the *USS Arizona* Memorial.

The former Naval Training Center in San Diego saw three buildings collectively renamed as the *John and Alice Finn Office Plaza* (after John and his beloved wife), and in 2012, an *Arleigh Burke-class destroyer* was also named in his honor.

John may have been a reluctant hero, but he embraced the love and adulation of his peers and never shied away from the important role he could play to inspire the next generation of servicemen.

Chapter 8:

William Wilbur

United States Army, Operation Torch, 1942

From the moment of landing until the cessation of hostile resistance, Col. Wilbur's conduct was voluntary and exemplary in its coolness and daring.
–President Franklin D. Roosevelt

Background of the Hero

William Wilbur was born on September 24, 1888, to Dr. and Mrs. John Wilbur. He grew up in the city of Palmer, Massachusetts and attended Springfield High School. William joined the Army after graduating from the United States Military Academy in West Point in 1912.

At the age of 24, William spent the first three years of military service in Panama, where he served as a second lieutenant and was primarily tasked with directing construction and the building of roads.

Showing natural leadership qualities, he soon transitioned back closer to home and spent the next three years as an instructor at the West Point Military Academy, where he'd completed his own training. His role as an instructor was to bestow leadership, calisthenics, and tactics to the latest classes of recruits.

William was progressing nicely and, as such, saw himself promoted to the rank of major in the American Expeditionary Forces in June 1918. It was at this point that William found himself commanding a battalion in France during World War I.

While in France he furthered his training by attending the French military academy *Ecole Speciale Militaire de Saint-Cyr and* graduated in 1920.

William was headed back home again, returning to an instructor role at the Infantry School in Fort Benning, Georgia. He'd teach for another two years before spending the next 15 years of his life traveling between the military academies of the United States and France, bolstering his know-how. He eventually graduated from the Army War College in 1935 and was promoted to the rank of lieutenant colonel.

With an array of leadership skills and hands-on experience in construction, tactics, and combat, William was to be a key player in the Second World War that was on the horizon. He served in Hawaii between the years 1935 and 1938, where he commanded the 1st Battalion, 35th Infantry for two years and took charge of war planning, civilian care, and controlling Japanese Americans.

By 1940, he had valiantly served his country for 28 years and was justly recognized by being promoted to colonel in November of that year. It would of course be the following years that would see William take the heroic action that earned him a place in this book, which we'll explore next.

The Heroic Act

After leading the 60th Infantry Regiment for a year, William was accepted to join the staff of General George Patton for the Moroccan action. His role was to be a key one, advising Patton on economic and political relations with the Moroccans and the French.

As a member of the Western Task Force, his mission was to help wrestle control of the Moroccan city of Casablanca from Vichy French forces. One way that America gained ground in Casablanca was by making contact with French commanders who were believed to be sympathetic to the Allied forces.

As one of the brave men tasked with carrying these messages, William would play a crucial role in Operation Torch on November 8, 1942. This operation resulted in America's first major victory of the war and secured North African footing for the Allies. Before that footing was established, however, inroads had to be made, and William was one of the men tasked with making them.

His goal was to deliver a letter from General Patton to the commander of the French naval forces, Admiral Francois Michelier. The Allies were hopeful that this could convince French commanders to lay down their guns.

Delivering the letter was going to be no easy task, and having landed with the first assault wave in the city of Fedala, William showed nerves of steel to approach enemy lines under a white flag. At that point, he was whisked off to the division headquarters. However, there was a problem: Admiral Michelier had been arrested for treason, and his presiding general had no interest in entertaining the request of General Patton.

William left the letter on the general's desk defiantly before being escorted back to his vehicle under the ominous arms of the Vichy French soldiers. He must have feared the worst when he was stopped in his tracks by a French officer, but the officer was an ally and wanted to take him to see Admiral Michelier.

Shaken by his arrest, Michelier refused to see William, and it appeared that a vital avenue into the city of Casablanca had evaporated in front of America's eyes.

With little option but to head back to the American lines in Fedala, it was during his drive back to the Allied-held beachhead that he spotted an enemy emplacement dealing heavy fire to an American landing site.

Without hesitation or regard for his own safety, William commandeered five approaching tanks and an attacking battalion, riding on the lead tank and using his tactical and leadership skills to capture the Vichy French troop's emplacement. This relieved the fire from his brothers landing on the beachhead and allowed them a safer inroad for the fight that was to come.

Operation Torch was eventually a success, and the stranglehold that the Axis powers had on West Africa was ripped from their hands. It's undeniable that William played a huge part in that success.

The Aftermath of the Act

Following his actions that day, William was promoted to brigadier general on December 1 and continued to serve valiantly throughout the rest of World War II. His service included fighting through the first five months of the Italian campaign, participating in the Allied landings in Salerno, and fighting throughout the winter of 1943 to 1944.

He was then stationed in east Asia in 1944, where he served for three years before retiring in 1947.

After his retirement, William continued to fight on a political front and gave speeches about the importance of withdrawing American troops from Korea throughout 1952. He would transition into a career in law enforcement and serve on the Chicago Crime Commission before taking up a post as a prison warden at Cook County Jail.

William died at age 91 and was buried at West Point Cemetery, in the grounds of the United States Military Academy.

A Lasting Legacy

Following his actions in Morocco, William was presented the Medal of Honor by President D. Roosevelt on the 22nd of January 1943. The ceremony fittingly took place in Casablanca and marked the first time that a U.S. President had presented the award to an American soldier outside of the United States.

His citation is as follows:

> For conspicuous gallantry and intrepidity in action above and beyond the call of duty. Col. Wilbur prepared the plan for making contact with French commanders in Casablanca and obtaining an armistice to prevent unnecessary bloodshed. On 8 November 1942, he landed at Fedala with the leading assault waves where opposition had developed into a firm and continuous defensive line across his route of advance. Commandeering a vehicle, he was driven toward the hostile defenses under incessant fire, finally locating a French officer who accorded him passage through the forward positions. He then proceeded in total darkness through 16 miles of enemy-occupied country intermittently subjected to heavy bursts of fire, and accomplished his mission by delivering his letters to appropriate French officials in Casablanca. Returning toward his command, Col. Wilbur detected a hostile battery firing effectively on our troops. He took charge of a platoon of American tanks and personally led them in an attack and capture of the battery. From the moment of landing until the cessation of hostile resistance, Col. Wilbur's conduct was voluntary and exemplary in its coolness and daring. (Wilbur, 2023)

William was also awarded the following (Wilbur, 2023):

- Bronze Star
- Silver Star
- Combat Infantryman Badge
- 2 x Legions of Merit
- Victory Medals for both World Wars that he fought in

Perhaps his greatest legacy, however, comes from his son, William Jr., who followed in his father's heroic footsteps and was posthumously awarded the Distinguished Service Cross after serving as a lieutenant.

William Wilbur bravely stepped behind enemy lines and acted quickly to prevent the deaths of countless American troops upon their arrival in Morocco. The part that he played in Operation Torch simply cannot be understated.

Chapter 9:

Virginia Hall

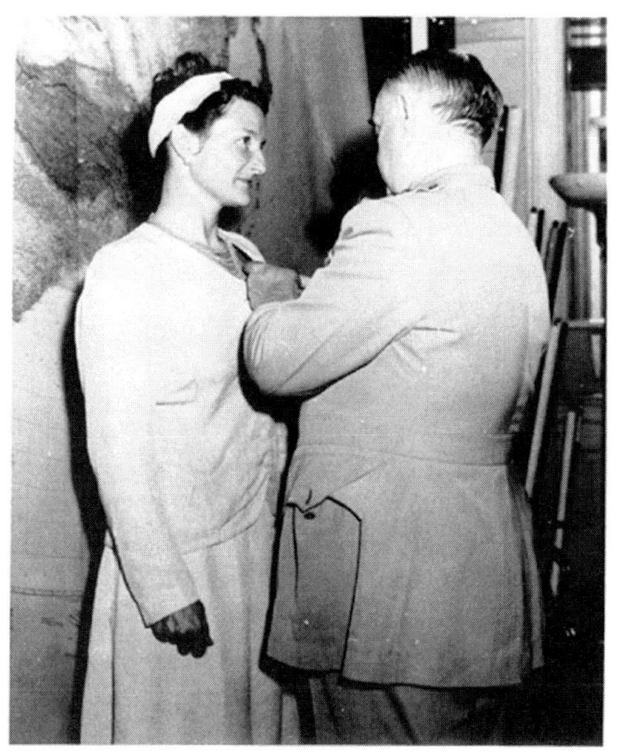

Special Operations Executive, Vichy France, 1941–1943

Many of my friends were killed for talking too much. –Virginia Hall

Background of the Hero

Virginia Hall was born in Baltimore, Maryland, in 1906, to parents Edwin Lee Hall and Barbara Virginia Hammel. Born into a life of privilege, her family's wealth never quite sat right with her. At a tender age, she wanted adventure and balked at the idea of marrying into her own privileged circle in the way her parents wished she would.

She was brave, quirky, and unique. When she attended Roland Park Country School, she once proudly went into school wearing a bracelet made of live snakes—far from the clean-cut young girl she was being raised to be!

After attending Roland Park Country School, she moved onto Radcliffe College of Harvard University, and then onto Barnard College of Columbia University before concluding her studies at George Washington University.

Her subjects of interest were French, Italian, German, and Economics—all subjects that provided her with an education incredibly useful in her future escapades. Virginia craved adventure and wanted to see the world, so her decision to complete her studies in Europe was no surprise.

Her travels took her to Austria, Germany, and France. She fell in love with the latter, and it was during her stint there that she would begin to shape her future. She wanted to be a diplomat, but her journey wasn't to be an easy one.

She was pushed back, belittled, and rejected constantly by the State Department in her pursuit to become a diplomat. Perhaps a sign of the time is that women only accounted for a meager six of the United States' 1,500 diplomats back then (Elder, 2016). She was fighting a losing battle, but fighting was something she was happy to do, and eventually saw her land her first role as a consular service clerk at the Embassy of the

United States in Warsaw in 1931—a role that saw her add Poland to her list of travel destinations. Seemingly unable to sit still, Virginia would shortly be on the move again, transferring to Turkey, where she would fulfill a similar role. It was in Turkey, however, that her life would take a detour, and her desire to fight would be truly tested.

In 1933, Virginia was out hunting birds when she tripped on a fence and suffered a horrific accident, shooting herself in the left foot. She suffered from gangrene and was at risk of losing her life had she not agreed to have her leg amputated below the knee.

Following surgery, she endured grueling rehabilitation that saw her learn how to use a clunky wooden leg that she named *Cuthbert*. She pushed herself through the physical and mental anguish of losing a limb and became determined to maximize the second chance at life that she'd been given. She was going to do great things and kick through the doors that were being closed in her face.

She initially continued work as a consular clerk in Italy and Estonia; all the while, she continued to try to take the relevant steps to become a diplomat with the United States Foreign Service, without success.

Unfortunately for Virginia, the hill that she was already climbing became much steeper when she stopped being just a woman and became a disabled woman. The year 1937 even saw her rejected by the Department of State because of a rule that prevented disabled people from being hired as diplomats (Hall, 2024).

Despite sending an appeal to Franklin D. Roosevelt, she couldn't find a way through the mire of discrimination and resigned from the Department of State in 1939. She was still desperate to make a difference and to make the most of her second chance. Ironically, World War II would present her with the chance to do just that. In February 1940, Virginia's love of France inspired her to volunteer as an ambulance driver for the French, thrusting herself into a conflict that wouldn't become her fellow Americans' problem until December of the following year.

Despite the efforts of Virginia and the French, they were soon defeated in June 1940. Virginia, however, wasn't ready to accept this and knew that her role in the war was far from over. Rather than returning to the relative sanctity of the United States, she stayed within Europe and traveled to Spain, where she would soon meet a British Intelligence officer.

It was at this point that her role in the Second World War would crystalize when she was put in touch with Nicolas Bodington, who was seeking help for the newly formed Special Operations Executive (SOE), a British organization formed in 1940 to conduct reconnaissance and sabotage, as well as aiding local resistance movements in German-occupied Europe.

The Heroic Act

After minimal training, Virginia officially joined the SOE in April 1941 and was deployed to Vichy France on August 23, 1941, as part of the SOE's F (France) Section. Posing as a reporter for the *New York Post,* she had free reign to interview people and gain intelligence that she could send back to Britain.

F Section was populated by 41 female agents, and by the end of the war, sadly only 26 would survive (Hall, 2024). Early casualties were inevitable, but Virginia kept her nerve even when many of those within her codenamed network of *Heckler* were arrested and killed. Based in Lyon, Virginia was cunning, clever, and smart. She used make-up and various outfits to remain completely inconspicuous and, at times, could don four different disguises within a single day. By taking advantage of the sexism of the Axis soldiers, who hadn't even considered that a woman could be a spy, let alone be one as devastating to their efforts as Virginia would grow to be, she was essentially able to become invisible.

She showed nerves of steel as she utilized a network of women from all walks of life. Initially, she stayed in a convent with nuns who agreed to help her; then she was able to befriend the owner of one of the city's most prominent brothels, which provided her access to any information that French prostitutes had been able to extract from Axis soldiers.

Virginia was even able to stay one step ahead of the Gestapo to organize bands of French resistance fighters and provide them with intelligence and safe houses.

One of her biggest assets in evading capture was her keen sense of danger and reliance on her intuition. She narrowly avoided capture in October 1941 when she avoided an ill-fated meeting with her fellow SOE agents in Marseille that resulted in the capture of a dozen of them.

The mass capture raised the stakes dramatically for both Virginia and the UK, as she was left as one of only a few agents with the means of transmitting information back to London.

She spent the end of 1941 locked within the precarious balancing act of extracting information and evading capture. All the while she was struggling to maintain her personal hygiene, at one point pleading with her SOE masters to send her some soap as her morale started to dip.

Still, she fought on, building new contacts and assisting in missions that saw her praised by the few peers that she would allow to get close to her. She would often refuse to work with contacts that she deemed unprofessional or untrustworthy and would allow her own intuition to dictate her decisions rather than direct orders from the SOE. Her male peers found her difficult to work with, not because of her lack of ability but for the simple fact that she was a female. Despite their chauvinistic reluctance, men were forced to work with and rely on her for one simple reason: She was damn good at what she did.

When a suspicious confidant asked her about *Cuthbert*, she slammed her wooden leg on the table with all the vigor you would expect, easing concerns and standing up for herself against her male counterparts.

One of Virginia's most perilous and important missions was rescuing British airmen who had been shot down over Europe and facilitating their rescue back to England via Spain. Downed airmen would ask to see "Oliver" at the American Consulate in France before being hidden by Virginia and her network (Purnell, 2019, p. 64).

Inevitably, Virginia's impact was so great that remaining invisible would become an impossible task.

The Germans would finally recognize that a limping lady had infiltrated them and put one of their most dangerous men on her tail: Klaus Barbie, or "*The Butcher of Lyon.*" Barbie's forces had already tortured and slaughtered thousands of people across France, and now our hero was in his sights.

Under Barbie's orders, posters of Virginia were plastered across France with the chilling words, "The Enemy's Most Dangerous Spy—We Must Find And Destroy Her!" (Myre, 2019).

The threat of the Axis and the Butcher did nothing to deter Virginia and instead appeared to pour gasoline on her internal fire. When she learned that the SOE agents captured in Marseille were being held in Mauzac prison, she couldn't let things lie.

Working alongside the wife of one of the 12 captors, Virginia helped to hatch a daring escape plan that would thrust herself into more danger at a time when the spotlight was shining on her the brightest.

While she was far too recognizable at this point to visit the prison herself, she helped conjure a plan that saw the prisoners smuggled sardine tins and tools that would eventually be used to foster a key to release them from their cells.

Virginia focused on assembling helpers, vehicles, and safe houses for the prisoners, who would eventually escape on July 15, 1942. The prisoners hid in the woods to withstand an intense manhunt, then joined Virginia in Lyon the next month, where she was able to secure them a safe return to England via Spain.

For Virginia to voluntarily take on the engineering of such a daring escape plan at a time when her own personal risk was at an all-time high seems unfathomable. But she selflessly embraced the task, and in doing so, saved the lives of all who had been captured.

I could forgive you for believing that we've reached the end of Miss Hall's heroism here, but she was far, far from finished.

With the Germans unsurprisingly enraged by the escape, they poured 500 agents into Vichy France, and their efforts to infiltrate and destroy the rising pockets of French resistance and SOE networks were dramatically increased.

Worryingly for Virginia, the Germans were focused on Lyon, having identified it as the nucleus of the resistance. Her contacts were also starting to dwindle as the German stranglehold tightened. She was coming under increased pressure, and made what was her first mistake in May 1942. Perhaps feeling the pressure of her dwindling contacts, Virginia agreed to have messages transmitted from a French resistance movement in Paris to the SOE in London. Just three months after her decision, the French resistance was infiltrated, and thus, so was her network of contacts.

The last straw for Virginia broke in November 1942 when the Allied invasion of North Africa prompted the Germans to occupy Vichy France, which left her with no choice but to flee Lyon. She went alone and told no one.

Surrounded by soldiers who saw her as their most wanted of targets, she was still able to pull off a daring escape from Lyon via a train to Perpignan, but the most grueling part of her journey was yet to come.

She was forced to drag her prosthetic leg behind her in an energy-sapping, 50-mile trek over the Pyrenees Mountains. She embarked on the trek in the dead of winter, forcing herself through heavy snow for three days.

Exhausted and sore, when she finally reached Spain, she was arrested because she did not have an entrance stamp on her passport, which was thankfully nothing compared to the fate that the Germans would have bestowed upon her.

After six weeks of imprisonment, the American Embassy was able to secure her release, and she would continue her work for the SOE in Madrid before returning to London in July 1943.

We've reached the second point in this incredible story, and indeed, if her story had ended here, she would still be very worthy of a place in this book and well-worth recognition as a brave hero.

However, Virginia still felt she had work to do.

Despite her desperation to return to France, Britain refused to send her back due to the fear that she was far too recognizable and that doing so would put her life at considerable risk.

Coincidentally, though, the Americans were endeavoring to ramp up an intelligence service of their own, called the *Office of Strategic Services* (OSS), and having very little presence in France, they knew that Virginia could be a major asset to them.

Naturally, Virginia was only happy to oblige despite the fact that she'd be joining the organization at the low rank and pay of a second lieutenant, whereas her actions thus far had surely earned more. However, she did not care for money or stature; she only wanted to help the French people who needed her.

Of course, there was still one major hurdle for her to clear: The German presence was rampant across France, and they were looking for her.

The only way for Virginia to return was in disguise. With a make-up artist's help, she learned how to draw wrinkles across her face, which she supplemented with dyed gray hair and filed down teeth to transform into an old French milkmaid. Her limp was disguised as an old woman's shuffle, and Virginia Hall became Marcelle Montagne, with a codename of Diane.

Virginia was truly fearless. On the 21st of March in 1944, she returned to the country that she'd so narrowly escaped with her life by motor gunboat alongside Henri Lassot, the man considered the leader of the new Saint network that Hall was to work within. The idea that a woman was capable of leading was still far too radical for the men of that time despite her accomplishments surely being greater than the majority.

The new Saint network's first objective was to train and arm other resistance groups needed to provide support for the Normandy Invasion. However, Virginia wasn't interested in objectives or Lassot's orders and was soon detached from the team to instead work under the guise of a milkmaid in the streets of southern Paris, with a French woman speaking for her to keep her accent a secret.

She was in deep, perhaps deeper than she'd ever been before, and would even sell cheese to German soldiers and listen in on their conversations. Meanwhile, she busied herself organizing drop zones, renewing old contacts, and fostering new ones. She also set to work establishing safe houses across Paris for those working to undermine the Germans.

Her work saw her organize resistance groups before supplying them with the arms to fight back. Despite engaging in several unsuccessful missions, including a failed jailbreak attempt, she was never deterred from her goal.

Under her leadership, French resistance groups dished out several small attacks on the German infrastructure and soldiers. She was chipping away at the Germans from the inside, creating chips that would soon splinter into major cracks.

In July 1944, Virginia abandoned her disguise and established a headquarters in a barn in south-central France. She was now tasked with sabotaging the Germans occupied in the South of France in anticipation of the Allies' Operation Dragoon.

Unfortunately for Virginia, when she arrived at the barn that was to be the heartbeat of her next venture, the misogyny that she'd faced throughout the war would rear its ugly head once more. As a woman with the rank of second lieutenant, she struggled to garner authority over the Maquis resistance groups and their leaders.

She was less than impressed with the OSS and complained that they had not provided her with the "necessary authority" to effectively undertake her task (Rossiter, 1986, pp. 196–197).

Like most of the men who had originally balked at the thought of working with her and greatly underestimated her, she would soon win them over when they were forced to begrudgingly accept that they needed her.

Virginia was extremely well connected by this point and agreed to finance the groups and provide them with weaponry as long as they agreed to take her advice. They agreed reluctantly, but things were far from smooth sailing. However, three planeloads of supplies and the cash she divided among the groups helped calm things down.

The three battalions she was advising were made of roughly 1,500 men, and she led them to multiple successful sabotage operations that harassed and pushed the Germans back.

Her work laid the groundwork for Operation Dragoon a month later, which was such a success that the German troops were forced to withdraw from Southern France completely. The chips had cracked, and Virginia's influence was undeniable.

Following the successful operation, Virginia returned to Paris before moving on to Austria to help rally and stir up the Anti-Nazi resistance fighters there, too. Once the Nazis had collapsed and her job was complete, Virginia then returned to Paris and set about writing recommendations of commendation for those that had helped her before resigning from the OSS.

It's no surprise that a woman who had so often been neglected of credit for her actions, was so staunch in her desire to credit others.

The Aftermath of the Act

Virginia was also sure to return to Lyon so that she could check on the welfare of some of her closest associates. She organized whatever monetary compensation that she could for those who had survived, which, sadly, were only a few from the network that had grown to more than 1,000 individuals at its peak. Most of her helpers would receive nothing, but I imagine escaping with their lives felt like the greatest gift.

When she returned home, Virginia was one of the first women hired by the CIA (Central Intelligence Agency) in 1947. Her time at the CIA was marred by more discrimination and sexism despite her incredible accomplishments (*Virginia Hall*, 2024).

Despite being ignored for honors and promotions, she worked diligently and did what she had always done: focused on helping people.

Her direct supervisors knew just how valuable an asset she was to the agency, though, and tasked her with gathering information on the Soviet penetration of the rest of Europe—a task that would see her mostly tied to her desk, clipping the wings that were so desperate to soar.

Throughout the 1950s, she performed the vital role of heading up top-secret paramilitary operations in her beloved France. She would then help several European countries prepare the formation of resistance groups in case of a Soviet attack.

Her stature was such that she became the first woman operations officer in the CIA's covert action arm and was absolutely vital in supporting undercover activities that undermined and prevented the growth of communism throughout Europe (*Virginia Hall*, 2024).

Gaining too much influence and acclaim for some of her male counterparts, it wouldn't be long until she was given a poor performance review from a superior who had never even worked with her.

The CIA has since admitted that Virginia faced discrimination and had been "sidelined" because she "threatened" and had experience that "overshadowed her male colleagues" (Purnell, 2019). Despite this, she endured the sexism and remained focused on her role until she retired from it at the mandatory age of 60, at which point she moved to a farm with the husband she had married in 1957, an OSS lieutenant.

Virginia passed away in 1982 at the age of 76, and she was buried in Maryland's Druid Ridge Cemetery.

A Lasting Legacy

Virginia Hall's incredible actions saw her awarded with the Distinguished Service Cross in 1945, the citation for which is included below:

> The President of the United States of America, authorized by Act of Congress, July 9, 1918, takes pleasure in presenting the Distinguished Service Cross to Miss Virginia Hall, a United States Civilian, for extraordinary heroism in connection with military operations against an armed enemy while serving as an American Civilian Intelligence Officer in the employ of the Special Operations Branch, Office of Strategic Services, who entered voluntarily and served in enemy-occupied France from March to September 1944.
>
> Despite the fact that she was well known to the Gestapo because of previous activities, Miss Hall established and maintained radio communications with London headquarters, supplying valuable operational and intelligence information. With the help of a Jedburgh team, she organized, armed, and trained three battalions of French resistance forces in the Department of the Haute Loire.
>
> Working in a region infested with enemy troops and continually at the risk of capture, torture, and death, she directed the resistance forces with extraordinary success in acts of sabotage and guerrilla warfare against enemy troops, installations, and communications. Miss Hall displayed rare courage, perseverance, and ingenuity.

> Her efforts contributed materially to the successful operations of the resistance forces in support of the Allied Expeditionary Forces in the liberation of France. (Hall, 2024)

She was the only civilian woman to receive the award (Hall, 2024).

I'd be remiss to neglect the fact that Virginia was awarded the prior accolade before she took the brave decision to join the OSS and return to France. She was never focused on accolades or awards; she simply wanted to make a difference. This is only substantiated further by her refusal of a public ceremony for the award because of the fact that she wanted to keep working. Her mother was the only public attendee.

She had also previously been quietly made an honorary member of the Order of the British Empire (MBE) in 1943, and was awarded the Croix de Guerre by France. In 1988, she was inducted into the inaugural class of the Military Intelligence Corps Hall of Fame.

Virginia was honored on the 100th anniversary of her birth in 2006 by both British and French ambassadors who came together in Washington. That same year, a CIA field agent training facility was also named in her honor.

She is one of only five operatives honored with a specific section in the CIA Museum's catalog and the only woman among them. In 2019, Virginia was an inductee of Maryland's Women's Hall of Fame.

One of the most incredible pieces of her legacy was perhaps her refusal to talk about her work even after retirement. She never spoke publicly about her work or sought acclaim, and when she returned from the war, her own niece attests that she "never talked about it" (Myre, 2019).

The 20th century saw an influx of projects that were unsurprisingly eager to tell her story. Several books have been written about her, and two movies have been released, as of 2024.

Virginia Hall showed unprecedented levels of courage, bravery, and cunning to undermine the Germans occupying France at every turn and risked her life for others. She was never interested in accolades or acclaim, but she deserves both.

Chapter 10:

Ruben Rivers

United States Army, Saar Campaign, 1944

I see 'em. We'll fight 'em! –Ruben Rivers

Background of the Hero

Ruben was born toward the climax of World War I, in October 1918, to African-American, working-class parents Lilian and Wille Rivers. He was born in the Oklahoma City of Tecumseh but primarily raised on his family's farm in the nearby town of Hotulka.

Ruben was one of 11 siblings, making it no surprise that he was a fighter. The siblings all pulled their weight on the farm, learning to work the heavy machinery, taking responsibility for its maintenance, and helping to raise the animals.

When Ruben graduated from high school in 1938, he found himself working on a local railroad. Like many other African Americans at that time, his employment options were limited, as was the likelihood of him reaching his potential.

While he might have been restricted by the glass ceiling that the color of his skin had built over him, he was undeterred in his quest to achieve greatness in his life. In October of 1940, Ruben registered for the United States Army draft, feeling that he could put his 6-foot-2-inch frame to good use.

It wouldn't be until January of 1942 that the Army would come calling, and Ruben would get his opportunity to fight for his country. But when he did, he grabbed it with both hands.

When Ruben and two of his brothers, whom he had registered alongside, were finally called upon, he was the only one of the trio assigned to a combat unit. He was promptly separated from his brothers, and I'm sure he was thinking about the unlikelihood of seeing them again as he reported for training with a tank battalion. His training saw him travel between Camps Claiborne, Livingston, and Polk in Louisiana before he was sent to Camp Hood in Texas.

Wherever he trained, the common denominator was the undeniable skill he showed across basic training and while operating both the M5 Stuart light tank and the M4 Sherman medium tank. Perhaps Ruben's experience operating heavy machinery on his family's farm had served him well, or maybe he was just a natural. Whatever the reason, Ruben was a very skilled tank driver, and those around him knew it.

Ruben's excellence at this time should also be quantified by the inevitable yet atrocious racism that he was forced to endure. He faced abuse from both the locals that he was serving to protect and the white soldiers that he was fighting alongside. Lesser men may have justifiably seen their spirits broken, but Ruben absorbed the abuse and focused on the mission - ironically, fighting back against the racist beliefs of Germany's Adolf Hitler.

Once Ruben passed his training with flying colors, he was assigned to the all-black 761st Tank Battalion. The battalion was nicknamed the *Black Panthers* and eventually placed under the jurisdiction of George S. Patton's Third Army.

The Heroic Act

It was on June 9, 1944, just three days removed from the Allies successful D-Day Invasion, that Ruben received the news that he would be shipping out to France as part of the 761st. With General Patton selecting the 761st as a key element of the Saar Campaign, his goal was to drive the Axis back to the Siegfried Line that separated France and Germany, and Ruben would eventually play a vital role in achieving Patton's goal.

After a period of additional training at Camp Shank in New York, Ruben, a Staff Sergeant by that time, boarded the *USS Esperance Bay* alongside the 761st and was headed to France, but not without a slight detour first.

Before heading to France, the *USS Esperance Bay* called into the United Kingdom so that the battalion could be kitted out with the newest model of the Sherman tank. This version, called the M4A3, boasted a 76mm gun, significantly more armor, and perhaps even more crucially, it was equipped with a new motor that allowed higher speeds to be traveled.

The benefit of that new motor was felt almost immediately when Ruben and the 761st landed on France's infamous Omaha Beach on October 1oth. The unit raced across 400 miles of the country in six short days to join the Third Army's attempts to break through the Siegfried Line, which was protecting the vital industrial sites of the Germans.

As the Allies strived to venture forth, their approach toward the commune of Vic-Sur-Seille was promptly halted by an ingeniously improvised roadblock that the Germans had created. Combining a fallen tree with deadly landmines, the Germans had not only halted the Allied forces, but they had also trapped them.

The Allies were sitting ducks in broad daylight, and the Germans soon began crashing mortars down on top of them among the piercing rounds from small arms.

Ruben, who was positioned in the lead tank, realized that following protocol wasn't going to prevent the inevitable bloodshed that would follow. So, he broke ranks to dismount from his tank in the face of rapid fire, skillfully avoided the scattered landmines, and wrapped a heavy cable around the fallen tree.

The rest of his unit watched on in astonishment as Ruben was able to evade enemy fire and return to his lead tank before ripping the tree from their path and allowing the Allied offensive to pour into Vic-Sur-Seille and capture the town, dealing a critical blow to the Axis.

Ruben's actions would posthumously see him awarded a Silver Star, the 761st's first, but his heroic acts were far from over, and the war was yet to be won.

With Vic-Sur-Seille captured, Ruben and the Allies progressed through France. It was just eight short days after he bravely lugged the tree aside on the 16th of November that our hero would go far beyond the call of duty once more and take action that ensured the Allies could deliver a victory.

Their next target was the German forces stationed around the town of Guébling, and Ruben took charge of the lead tank once more. As he led the way, he was met by fields and roads scattered with the ominous shells of Allied tanks that had tried, and failed, to infiltrate the town in previous attacks.

Despite this, Ruben led the Black Panthers defiantly toward their target. The 11 tanks of the Able Company tactically split into two groups on approach, with Ruben leading one of them.

As Ruben's group crested a rise, they were met by a wave of heavy German artillery that caused severe damage and disabled one of his tanks. Undeterred, Ruben pressed forth, penetrating the town despite his captain's warning that it was too dangerous. Much to Ruben's captain's shock, he revealed that he had already made it into the town.

Ruben's tank was shortly stopped in its tracks by an anti-tank mine that ripped through it with such force that it blew him from the tank and nearly flipped the entire vehicle on its side.

His brothers fought on, spilling into the town in the face of heavy fire, and when medics were finally able to reach Ruben, they found him in dire straits. He had valiantly dragged himself behind the shelter of his disabled tank, but the shrapnel from the blast had callously torn right through his leg all the way from his thigh to his knee, right through to his bone.

Ruben had no choice but to try and agonizingly hold his wound shut with his hands, and the call was promptly made to mercifully evacuate Ruben back to Tecumseh. What Ruben did next is shocking even by the bar set previously in this book. He refused evacuation despite his leg having been torn open.

Before a medic could plunge the sweet relief of a morphine needle into his leg, Ruben knocked it aside and refused a direct order from his sergeant before dragging himself to his feet.

Ruben had sacrificed more than his fair share, but he was going nowhere, telling his superior that this would be the "only order" that he'd "ever disobey," but that they "needed him," and he had a war to win (*Platoon Sergeant Ruben Rivers and the 761st Tank Battalion*, 2020).

After being patched up as well as the medics could manage, Ruben knocked past his superior defiantly and ignored the stretcher awaiting him. Instead, with gritted teeth and adrenaline pumping through his veins, he stumbled over to another tank and ordered the men within it out.

Before another word could be exchanged, German mortar resumed thundering upon them, and Ruben was right back in the fight behind the controls of a tank, doing his best to protect the ground men who had been forced to scatter for shelter.

Gangrene was quickly settling into Ruben's wound, and the combination of the blood loss and the infection was sapping his energy. Still, he spent the night providing cover for combat engineers, erecting a bridge to allow them entry to the town of Guébling.

The Germans forced Ruben and the Allies to fight hard, and with Ruben leading the way, they crossed the bridge and engaged in heavy fire. Despite his dwindling energy, he was right at the front and engaged enemy tanks and gunners, even managing to prevent German soldiers donning the uniforms of

American prisoners from infiltrating their unit. With his leg swelling and energy levels running on empty, it was on the following day that Ruben would perform his final, defiantly heroic act.

On the 19th of November, the Blank Panthers would make one more brave attempt to break the lines at Guébling, with the wounded Ruben right at the helm.

This time, however, the Germans were waiting with anti-tank weaponry that would carve through the Allied tanks.

Knowing that his brothers were facing certain death, Ruben ordered that his tank leave the cover that it had taken and sacrificed himself so that his brothers could retreat safely. Ruben's tank engaged the enemy, sending shells desperately toward them despite the cries of his superiors to retreat.

Ruben didn't have an ounce of quit in him and fought back for long enough for his brothers to find safety. Finally, Ruben's tank was struck by German artillery, and the tank erupted into flames.

Ruben and the crew that fought so valiantly beside him were killed instantly.

The Aftermath of the Act

Ruben's sacrifice was vital for the progression of the Black Panthers, who not only took the town, but then defiantly marched onwards to the Battle of the Bulge, where they would also play a key part in another critical Allies' victory.

Ruben was fittingly buried in France's Second World War Military Cemetery, Lorraine American Cemetery and Memorial.

A Lasting Legacy

Ruben was awarded a Silver Star for his incredible removal of the fallen tree; his citation reads:

> During the daylight attack ... Staff Sergeant Rivers, a tank platoon sergeant, was in the lead tank when a roadblock was encountered which held up the advance. With utter disregard for his personal safety, Staff Sergeant Rivers courageously dismounted from his tank in the face of directed enemy small arms fire, attached a cable to the road block and moved it off the road, thus permitting the combat team to proceed. His prompt action thus prevented a serious delay in the offensive action and was instrumental in the successful assault and capture of the town. His brilliant display of initiative, courage and devotion to duty reflect the highest credit upon Staff Sergeant Rivers and the armed forces of the United States. (Rivers, 2022)

Ruben was also posthumously awarded the Medal of Honor. He was initially scheduled to receive the honor on November 20, 1944. Unfortunately, due to the racial discrimination prevalent at the time, it would take another 50 years for him to be presented with the honor.

President Bill Clinton presented the honor to Ruben's sister, Grace Woodfolk, in 1997, and the citation read:

> For conspicuous gallantry and intrepidity at the risk of his life above and beyond the call of duty: Staff Sergeant Rivers distinguished himself by extraordinary heroism in action during 16-19 November 1944, while serving with Company A, 761st Tank Battalion. On 16 November 1944, while advancing toward the town of Guébling, France, Staff Sergeant Rivers' tank hit a mine at a railroad crossing.

> Although severely wounded, his leg slashed to the bone, Staff Sergeant Rivers declined an injection of morphine, refused to be evacuated, took command of another tank, and advanced with his company into Guébling the next day. Repeatedly refusing evacuation, Staff Sergeant Rivers continued to direct his tank's fire at enemy positions beyond the town through the morning of 19 November 1944.
>
> At dawn that day, Company A's tanks advanced toward Bourgaltoff, their next objective, but were stopped by enemy fire. Captain David J. Williams, the Company Commander, ordered his tanks to withdraw and take cover. Staff Sergeant Rivers, however, radioed that he had spotted the German antitank positions: "I see 'em. We'll fight 'em!" Staff Sergeant Rivers, joined by another Company A tank, opened fire on enemy tanks, covering Company A as they withdrew.
>
> While doing so, Staff Sergeant Rivers' tank was hit, killing him and wounding the rest of the crew. Staff Sergeant Rivers' fighting spirit and daring leadership were an inspiration to his unit and exemplify the highest traditions of military service. (Rivers, 2022)

Ruben was only one of seven African Americans to be awarded the Medal of Honor for their actions throughout the Second World War.

Ruben also posthumously received the following awards (*Ruben Rivers*, n.d.):

- Purple Heart
- World War II Victory Medal

Outside of his military accomplishments, there is also a court in El Paso, Texas, and a barracks in Germany named in his honor. In 2006, Ruben was inducted into the Oklahoma Military Hall of Fame.

Ruben Rivers exhausted every last ounce of fight his body would afford him to ensure his unit marched onwards to the Battle of the Bulge. He paid the ultimate sacrifice and should never be forgotten.

Chapter 11:

George Walters

Civilian, Pearl Harbor, 1941

He was trying to hit the planes. And he was pointing at the planes so the ships below can see the planes coming. –Lewis Walters (son of George)

Background of the Hero

Many of the heroes you'll read about in this book went above and beyond the call of duty. However, George Walters is a man who took it upon himself to make the duty his own.

George was not a soldier, and he had not made the decision to fight for his country or lay his life on the line—at least not until the morning of December 7, 1941.

George was born in Denver, Colorado, but his parents moved to Hawaii when he was just 14 months old. It was in Hawaii that he was raised to be a truly caring, empathetic, and selfless person—three attributes that would form the bedrock needed to perform an act of true heroism.

Before George put his life on the line for others, he volunteered at a children's hospital, where he sacrificed hours of his time to perform as a ringmaster and clown for sick children as part of the Shriner clown group, a charitable group that had one goal: to put smiles on the faces of those that needed it.

Shriners wasn't his only charitable venture and was supplemented with other volunteer work in a range of different guises.

In his private life, George's interests were fittingly rooted in his ability to empathize and care. He loved to grow things, learned to make compost, and discovered how to install an irrigation system. He was a tinkerer and very good with his hands, as well as possessing the ability to think on his feet and come up with solutions considered outside the box.

This brings us neatly to his decision to become a crane operator in Pearl Harbor in 1935, which was precisely what he was doing on the morning that the Japanese arrived.

The Heroic Act

The morning of the attack on Pearl Harbor, workers and soldiers would be forgiven for feeling disoriented and scared and for running for their lives.

George had a slightly different, albeit more terrifying, view of the Japanese bombers converging on Pearl Harbor that morning: He was 50 feet up in the air in the cab of the crane that he operated for a living!

He had a view that gave him time to scramble to safety, but instead, he made the split-second decision to stand 50 feet tall and fight for his country.

Crucially, his crane was positioned alongside the dry dock where the *USS Pennsylvania* had been undergoing maintenance—maintenance that George himself was actually contributing to. Little did he know that he would become the only defense between the vulnerable ship and the relentless planes of the Japanese.

When the first bombs erupted, it didn't take George long to realize that the Japanese were racing toward the majestic ship below him. Fearing for the men obliviously working on her, he desperately tried to get their attention by waving the crane's arm erratically.

George had unexpectedly become the workers' last line of defense. First, he swung the crane's arm in an attempt to block the aerial attacks. Then, he quite literally started pointing out the points of attack for the Americans on the ground. Although they were initially confused and disorientated by the crane's erratic swinging, those that were initially struggling to fire back at their Japanese attackers soon realized that the crane's movements were far more deliberate than they'd first seemed.

They were being guided and warned.

With George's assistance, not only were the Americans able to defend themselves, but they also started to fight back and dished out devastating losses to their Japanese attackers.

George slammed the controls of the crane with vigor and determination to protect not only the *USS Pennsylvania,* but he became sick of playing defense and started fighting back by swiping the arm of the crane at the airborne attackers!

A combination of George's clever swatting and the ship's crew operating the *Pennsylvania's* weaponry were able to down at least 10 enemy fighters and disorient them enough that the ship survived the attack.

George fought long and hard until his crane was finally targeted by Japanese bombers, and he had a 500-pound bomb dropped on his location. Despite getting his crane out of the way seconds before what would have been a fatal blast, the explosion left a 17-foot crater in its wake and knocked him out cold.

At that point, it was the turn of the officers on the ground to return the favor for George, and they happily obliged. A Navy officer climbed up to the crane's cabin and tackled its heroic operator to the floor, surely saving his life just before a bomb ripped through the vicinity.

When George later pondered his survival, he questioned why "God" had "protected him" but felt sure that he must have "had a reason" (Morse, 1999).

Incredibly, his crane is even credited with destroying one of the enemy planes, which is believed to have become tangled in the crane's cables before crashing into a nearby building.

Perhaps one of the most incredible elements of George's heroism that day is that one of the many shipyard workers also in attendance and scrambling around for cover below him was his son, Lewis. When remarking on what he had seen his dad do that day, Lewis simply stated that his father was a "fighter" (Mendoza, 2019).

The Aftermath of the Act

After his heroic actions, George continued operating the crane that he wielded with such bravery until 1950, at which point he continued on at Pearl Harbor shipyard until his retirement in 1966.

George passed away in 1999 at the age of 95.

A Lasting Legacy

Although he wasn't eligible to receive military recognition, in 1994, George was chosen as the outstanding male citizen as part of Salt Lake City Mayor Deedee Corradini's Senior Recognition Program.

I'm sure that George was proud of his award, but his greatest legacy comes from his three children, 12 grandchildren, and 20 great-grandchildren who were able to live in a free world.

George's bravery helped to prevent the Japanese from blowing up the *USS Pennsylvania* and inflicting even more losses on the American troops that day.

Chapter 12:

Frank Peregoy

United States Army, Normandy Invasion, 1944

The extraordinary gallantry and aggressiveness displayed by Technical Sargeant Peregory are exemplary of the highest tradition of the armed forces. –Warner Cable

Background of the Hero

Frank Peregoy was born on April 10, 1916, in Virginia. His parents, James and Susan, struggled to make ends meet, and as such, Frank grew up in an impoverished setting. One of the reasons that his family may have struggled is the sheer number of mouths that needed feeding, with Frank being the second oldest of 11 children.

Sadly, the two youngest of Frank's siblings died as infants, and his older sibling died, too, leaving him with the responsibility of being the oldest surviving member of a family that was reeling from the heartache of loss.

By 1930, Frank's father was running a small farm in Albemarle County, which Frank helped on with the rest of his siblings. Things were running smoothly despite the chaos that surely came with eight siblings working together!

That was until 1931, when disaster struck the Peregoy family again. While pregnant with her 12th child, Frank's mother contracted influenza, and neither she nor the baby survived the illness.

The death of his mother had a big impact on Frank's life that far exceeded the emotional anguish that he was wracked with. Now, his father was alone and needed to raise eight children by himself.

As the oldest, Frank took the responsibility of quitting school to help his father raise and support his siblings. The responsibility and sacrifice that his decision took are themes that will recur throughout his journey from impoverished farm worker to World War II hero. Having left school to help provide for his siblings, Frank needed a job fast. His first port of call was joining the Virginia National Guard in Charlottesville, where he joined Company K (Monticello

Guard), 116th Infantry, 29th Division (Kutch, n.d.). At just 15 years of age, Frank was too young to enlist at the time, so he was forced to lie about his age. It was during this enlisting that his surname was also written incorrectly as "Peregory," and that misspelling was then used throughout his military records moving forward. I imagine he feared that bringing attention to his wrongly spelled name may also do so to his falsified age.

In 1935, tragedy struck the Peregoy family yet again when Frank's father was found dead after several days spent drinking heavily. At the age of just 19, Frank found himself the breadwinner for his seven younger siblings after all of them had been made orphans before they could reach adulthood.

Frank kept his head down and worked hard for the Virginia National Guard for the next six years until his life took another sharp, unexpected turn on February 3, 1941. On that date, the Monticello Guard was mobilized into Federal service in anticipation of the United States' involvement in World War II—Frank was going to war.

Frank had achieved the rank of private first class at that time and was among 92 men who were sent to Maryland for training. When he was sent home for a break from his yearlong training course, he took the opportunity to marry his girlfriend, Bessie Kirby, and the two wed on July 5, 1941.

The Heroic Act

Frank was stationed in Fort Meade as part of the 29th Division and stepped up his training for the war.

On January 10, 1942, Frank and the members of the 116th Infantry were in transit through North Carolina when their patrol truck slid from an icy road and plunged into a deep canal.

With three men unable to free themselves and at risk of drowning, two brave men jumped into action and were able to rescue two of them. The third man, however, had been knocked unconscious and submerged with the vehicle.

In dire straits, Frank volunteered to rescue the man from the freezing water and promptly sliced a hole in the top of their truck before diving in not once, but twice, and emerging with the body of his unconscious brother.

The rescue took so much out of Frank that when he went for help with a small group, he had to complete the end of the journey on his hands and knees. With the frozen clothes stuck tight to his skin and his tired limbs dragging behind him, Frank and his brothers were able to get help for the rest of those in the crash.

For his part in the rescue, Frank received the highest non-combat award a soldier could have bestowed upon him: the Soldier's Medal.

As heroic as Frank's actions were that day, it's not that action that saw him included in this publication. He was still to be further tested in ways that he never believed possible.

Before those further tests, though, he would be sent overseas, where he would undergo two years of further training with the 29th. He was then promoted to the rank of technical sergeant before the 29th were selected to join the Regular Army's 1st Infantry Division for an assault on one of the Axis' five fortified beaches. Their target was the French beach codenamed "Omaha."

Frank was to play a key role in the Allies' success on D-Day.

First, he landed on June 6 and found himself caught in the frantic, frenetic bloodshed of being among the first wave of troops to land on Omaha Beach. He surged up out of the heavy ocean and fought his heavy legs to advance through the bloody sand, with heavy Axis machineguns cutting through more than 800 of his brothers around him and mortar shells crashing down on them ferociously from the Maisy Battery line of defenses.

Forced to stagger over the bodies of his fallen brothers and at a severe disadvantage because of the advantageous position of the Axis across the steep embankments of the beach, survival looked nearly impossible for Frank, but he lived through *Bloody Omaha* to see another day.

Frank and the surviving Allies hadn't just survived, but they had managed to thrive, and by June 8, they had reached the outskirts of the town of Grandcamp-Maisy, a key stronghold for the Axis.

The Axis still had the high ground, though, making the Allies' advancement through the town extremely dangerous. Despite the attempts of Allied tanks and artillery fire to nullify their threat from above, their attempts were ineffective, and the Allies were sitting ducks for an aerial barrage.

At this point, Frank's willingness to sacrifice his own needs for those of the people around him presented itself once more when he ventured up the hill on his own in the face of torrential fire.

Once he'd reached the hill's crest, he spotted an entrenchment that led to the Axis' main fortifications some 200 yards away. Knowing he had a chance to strike at the heart of their defenses, Frank dropped down into the trench and progressed relentlessly toward said heart.

His progression wasn't without the presence of Axis troops, of course, but when he first stumbled across an Axis squad of 11 strong, he used his cunning, strength, and skillful combination of his bayonet and hand grenades to slash and blow through eight of the enemy before the remaining three surrendered. He continued onwards with his head high and chest puffed—engaging in hand-to-hand combat, tearing through tired flesh with the business end of his bayonet and dispatching grenades to disperse larger groups of soldiers.

Frank had torn through the trenches and the German defenses like a one-man wrecking crew. When all was said and done, Frank staggered through more than 200 yards of trenches to reach the German fortifications and forced the surrender of more than 32 Germans in the process (Peregory, 2024).

With reprieve from the defensive bombardment, Frank's battalion were able to advance on the town of Grandcamp-Maisy and secure their objective.

The Aftermath of the Act

Frank personally played a key role in the Allies' successful invasion of Normandy on D-Day, which subsequently enabled them to liberate Western Europe and bring World War II to an end.

Sadly, Frank would be killed in action just six short days later on June 14, 1944. He was buried in the Normandy American Cemetery, which poignantly overlooks the Omaha Beach that he braved so valiantly.

A Lasting Legacy

For his heroic actions, Frank would receive the Medal of Honor posthumously in June of 1945, awarded to his wife, Bessie.

His citation reads:

> On 8 June 1944, the 3rd Battalion of the 116th Infantry was advancing on the strongly held German defenses at Grandcamp-Maisy, France, when the leading elements were suddenly halted by decimating machine gun fire from a firmly entrenched enemy force on the high ground overlooking the town. After numerous attempts to neutralize the enemy position by supporting artillery and tank fire had proved ineffective, T/Sgt. Peregory, on his own initiative, advanced up the hill under withering fire, and worked his way to the crest where he discovered an entrenchment leading to the main enemy fortifications 200 yards away.
>
> Without hesitating, he leaped into the trench and moved toward the emplacement. Encountering a squad of enemy riflemen, he fearlessly attacked them with hand grenades and bayonet, killed 8 and forced 3 to surrender. Continuing along the trench, he single-handedly forced the surrender of 32 more riflemen, captured the machine gunners, and opened the way for the leading elements of the battalion to advance and secure its objective. The extraordinary gallantry and aggressiveness displayed by T/Sgt. Peregory are exemplary of the highest tradition of the armed forces. (Stories of Sacrifice, n.d.)

By the end of World War II, Frank had also been awarded (Peregory, 2024):

- Combat Infantryman Badge
- Purple Heart
- Soldier's Medal

- Army Good Conduct Medal
- American Defense Service Medal
- European-African-Middle Eastern Campaign Medal with one bronze campaign star and an Arrowhead device
- American Campaign Medal
- World War II Victory Medal

Outside of Frank's military accomplishments, he had a building complex in Virginia dedicated to him in 1984, and a monument was erected to accompany the complex that described the brave actions that led to him being awarded both a Soldier's Medal and the Medal of Honor.

There is also a reserve and a fitness center named in his honor, and the street that houses the Virginia National Guard Armory has been renamed Peregory Lane—before it was later renamed in 2016 to feature the correct spelling of his name.

Frank Peregoy tore through German entrenchments with such aggression and skill that he single-handedly allowed his brothers to march on to the town of Grandcamp-Maisy.

Chapter 13:

Leo Powers

This image has been used with the kind permission of the Congressional Medal of Honor Society.

United States Army, Battle of Monte Cassino, 1944

I was just mad, I guess. –Leo J. Powers

Background of the Hero

Leo Powers was born on April 5, 1909. He was raised in the tiny farming town of Anselmo in Nebraska, which had 351 inhabitants at the time (Hoarn, 2014). Leo sadly lost his parents at a tender age and only received eight years of formal schooling, meaning his education was mostly learned outside and working with his hands.

Along with the rest of the town's minimal inhabitants, he worked on the local farms and became very good with his hands early on through tinkering and learning how to create things. One of the things that Leo decided to build with all that time on his hands was bombs, which unsurprisingly got him in trouble with the law.

When he was 23, the police raided his house and found shotguns and a pistol (neither of which were uncommon in rural Nebraska), but what they were really concerned with were the explosives that he'd built to blow up snowbanks.

Working as a washing machine mechanic at the time, the only thing that Leo was actually guilty of was seeking some excitement to contrast his menial job—excitement that he found by blowing things up!

He wasn't charged, and in September 1942, he would find himself drafted into the United States Army. It wasn't smooth sailing for Leo, though, and he was originally not considered fit to fight due to wearing dentures (a bizarre rule of the time).

However, he was able to convince the officers otherwise due to his desperation to see combat. After all, Leo was already very comfortable handling guns and explosives, so why wouldn't he want to put those skills to good use in defending his country?

A combination of Leo being 32 when he enlisted—older than the 26-year-old average of soldiers at the time—and the dentures that he wore meant that it didn't take long for his brothers to affectionately nickname him "Pop" (Hoarn, 2014).

He initially served on the front lines, but when he contracted trench foot, he was instead withdrawn to work as a mechanic, putting all of the time he'd spent tinkering on farms to good use.

The Allies would become desperate in 1944, however, when they started suffering heavy losses during the Battle of Monte Cassino. The loss was so great, in fact, that three battalions of the 133rd Infantry Regiment lost more than half of its soldiers (Hoarn, 2014).

The Allies were bleeding, and desperate times called for desperate measures. Leo, having previously been considered unfit for combat due to his foot issues, was called upon to join the weakened 133rd Infantry Regiment, 34th Division.

The Heroic Act

On February 3, 1944, Leo's company was dispatched. However, their chances of success looked as slim as they were grim. Their mission was to seize Hill 175, which was integral to the German's control of Cassino, Italy.

Its importance meant that it was fortified by 50 soldiers, three pillboxes housing heavy machine guns, and mortar fire that would rain down on any Allies that approached it from the cover of a steep hill.

Unsurprisingly, Leo and his company soon faced the same fate that their brothers had and were suffering heavy casualties as they desperately tried to ascend the hill toward their attackers.

Their progress was halted, and they found themselves completely pinned down. Soon, they had lost eight soldiers, and more deaths looked inevitable until Leo showed incredible bravery and heroism to take action that would turn the tide.

Despite the rattling of heavy machine gun fire, the relentless peppering of small German arms, and mortar shells relentlessly crashing down on them from above, Leo decided to ascend the hill alone.

Pressing his stomach to the sodden grass, he crawled toward the closest of the trio of pillboxes, getting to within just 15 yards of it. At that point, knowing that he had very little chance of survival even if his mission was successful, he rose triumphantly in the face of an avalanche of fire, reached back, and launched one of the four grenades hanging from his belt into the first pillbox.

His grenade rattled into it with precision, exploding with a sickening crack that took the lives of two and saw four more scramble despite their heavy wounds. The rattling of one of the machine guns had finally been silenced, and the Allies were able to press forward temporarily.

That was until a second pillbox scythed bullets across the Allies from the left-hand side, forcing them to halt and take cover once more.

Leo, back on his stomach and well isolated from the rest of his company, began another steep crawl toward the second pillbox, dragging his tired limbs and disabled foot behind him and getting as close as 15 feet once more.

Again, he rose tall in the face of the symphonic fire, ripped the pin of a grenade in his teeth, and tossed it into the pillbox with incredible accuracy. His toss silenced the pillbox, killed one more soldier, and saw another four scrambling for their lives.

Many might have considered their job done at that point, but for Leo, there was one more objective for him to conquer. With adrenaline pumping through his veins and the lives of his brothers on his shoulders, he set his sights on the third and final pillbox.

He repeated the trick, but this time, he was peppered by the fire of soldiers who had now become acutely aware of his presence. Despite the fire, Leo was able to roll quickly and make himself an impossible target until he was within 10 yards once more.

For the third and final time, Leo took the deepest of breaths, dragged himself to his feet, and almost dared the enemy to hit him as he tossed not one but two grenades into the third pillbox.

The jangling of the final heavy machine gun fell silent, and the crack of the grenade against the metal walls indicated the death of two more Axis soldiers. Four more scrambled out, heavily wounded, and quickly surrendered to their conqueror.

Triumphantly, Leo returned to his company with his four prisoners, having single-handedly broken the foundations of a vital Axis position. Leo and his company progressed through to the city of Cassino and, eventually, Rome, which drew the Germans away from the Soviet Union and provided an important distraction so that the Allies could finalize their D-Day plans.

The Aftermath of the Act

By the end of the Second World War, Leo had reached the rank of sergeant. Once he had completed his service, he returned home and continued to work as a sheep farmer. He lived until he was 58 years old and was buried in the Holy Cross Cemetery in Butte, Montana, following his death on July 14, 1967.

A Lasting Legacy

The courage that Leo showed during Monte Cassino saw him awarded the Medal of Honor in 1945 following two days of sightseeing in Washington, D.C., alongside his family; his citation is as follows:

> For conspicuous gallantry and intrepidity at risk of life above and beyond the call of duty. On 3 February 1944, this soldier's company was assigned the mission of capturing Hill 175, the key enemy strong point northwest of Cassino, Italy. The enemy, estimated to be at least 50 in strength, supported by machineguns emplaced in 3 pillboxes and mortar fire from behind the hill, was able to pin the attackers down and inflict 8 casualties.
>
> The company was unable to advance, but Pfc. Powers, a rifleman in 1 of the assault platoons, on his own initiative and in the face of the terrific fire, crawled forward to assault 1 of the enemy pillboxes which he had spotted. Armed with 2 hand grenades, and well aware that if the enemy should see him it would mean almost certain death, Pfc. Powers crawled up the hill to within 15 yards of the enemy pillbox. Then standing upright in full view of the enemy gunners in order to throw his grenade into the small opening in the roof, he tossed a grenade into the pillbox.
>
> At this close, the grenade entered the pillbox, killed 2 of the occupants and 3 or 4 more fled the position, probably wounded. This enemy gun silenced, the center of the line was able to move forward again, but almost immediately came under machinegun fire from a second enemy pillbox on the left flank. Pfc. Powers, however, had located this pillbox, and crawled toward it with absolutely no cover if the enemy should see him.

> Raising himself in full view of the enemy gunners about 15 feet from the pillbox, Pfc. Powers threw his grenade into the pillbox, silencing this gun, killing another German and probably wounding 3 or 4 more who fled. Pfc. Powers, still acting on his own initiative, commenced crawling toward the third enemy pillbox in the face of heavy machine-pistol and machinegun fire. Skillfully availing himself of the meager cover and concealment, Pfc. Powers crawled up to within 10 yards of this pillbox fully exposed himself to the enemy gunners, stood upright and tossed the 2 grenades into the small opening in the roof of the pillbox.
>
> His grenades killed 2 of the enemy and 4 more, all wounded, came out and surrendered to Pfc. Powers, who was now unarmed. Pfc. Powers had worked his way over the entire company front, and against tremendous odds had single-handedly broken the backbone of this heavily defended and strategic enemy position, and enabled his regiment to advance into the city of Cassino. Pfc. Powers' fighting determination and intrepidity in battle exemplify the highest traditions of the U.S. Armed Forces. (Powers, n.d.)

He called the three days he spent in D.C. with his family, culminating in the award, the "biggest three-day thrill" he'd ever had (Hoarn, 2014).

While information regarding Leo's other awards and accolades is hard to source, we know that he also received a World War II winners medal alongside his Medal of Honor.

Leo Powers showed incredible bravery to pave the way for his brothers to march on to the city of Cassino, where another major victory was soon to come.

Chapter 14:

Louis Zamperini

United States Air Force, the Pacific Island of Funafuti, 1941-1945

However dark the night, however dim our hopes, the light will always follow darkness. –Louis Zamperini

Background of the Hero

Louis Zamperini was born in Olean, New York in 1917. His parents, Louise Dossi and Anthony Zamperini, were both Italian natives and devout Catholics who raised Louis, his older brother, and his two younger sisters in an extremely strict manner.

Having moved to the United States from Italy, his family would bounce around a little bit when Louis was a baby. They moved from New York to California and then settled in Torrance in 1919. Louis faced many challenges as a child, nearly losing his life twice—once from almost drowning after falling into an oil rig and the other time by narrowly escaping a house fire.

Like many children who were raised in a strict environment, Louis soon rebelled against his parents' wishes and started drinking and smoking at a very tender age. He was rebellious, spunky, and aggressive throughout his time at Torrance High School, where he was initially bullied due to not speaking the language.

Needing to turn the tide on his tormentors, Louis' father decided to teach him boxing so that he could defend himself, and boy, did he. Once equipped with boxing lessons, Louis was able to get even with the children who had tormented him and relished the fights that he would find himself thrust into.

He was a brave fighter from a young age, a quality that would serve him well in the future. But in the present, he was veering off the rails as he became addicted to the daily fights.

He soon added prankster and thief to his list of early misdemeanors and desperately needed direction. That direction would be offered to him by his older brother, who invited him to join the high school track team that he was already a key part of.

Fueled by the desire to prove his bullies wrong, having previously been humiliated by coming dead last in a footrace with them, Louis accepted his brother's challenge.

To the delight of both Louis and his brother, he was a natural. He took to running quickly and was getting faster with every training run. Training typically took form in the shape of Louis being chased by his brother on a bicycle and hitting him in the legs with a stick. As unorthodox as the technique might have been, it was effective. Plus, with his focus away from fighting, Louis was maturing and showing a real talent for running.

He was soon drawn to Glenn Cunningham, a highly successful American runner who would end his career as one of the country's greatest ever. With Cunningham as his role model and his brother in his corner, Louis took up long-distance running and finished fifth in the All-City C-Division 660-yard dash at the end of his freshman year.

Louis was fueled by the newfound respect that he was gaining from the classmates that used to ridicule him, and children that previously didn't even know his name started calling him by it and wanting to talk to him (Hillenbr, 2010).

He had a problem, though, in that he had reached somewhat of a crossroads: If he was really serious about running, then he would have to cut down on smoking and drinking, a fact that his older brother was only too keen to point out.

With his brother's words ringing in his ears, Louis spent the summer of 1932 so fanatical about running that he wouldn't even indulge himself with as little as a milkshake—he was all in.

Following that, Louis spent the next three years undefeated in high school track and even started to surpass some of his older brother's records.

In 1934, he was able to set an interscholastic record for the mile, and the very next week, he won the CIF California State Meet championship. His notoriety was rising, so much so that he earned a scholarship to study at the University of Southern California (*Louis Zamperini*, 2019).

It was while still enrolled at the university that Louis made the decision to try out for the 1936 Summer Olympics in Berlin, Germany. At this point, he and the rest of the world were blissfully unaware of the impact that Germany was going to have on their future.

Back then, athletes had to pay to try out for the competition, which posed a problem for Louis, whose family didn't have the financial means. Despite that lack of means, from the combination of a free rail ticket from his father, who worked on the railroad, and the fundraising efforts of Torrance locals, Louis was on his way to the Olympic trials.

The locals were so supportive of Louis that they gathered to see him off before he left for New York and presented him with a suitcase filled with new clothes and a wallet bursting with money for his travels. Long before the heroic act that earned Louis a place in this publication, he was a local hero in his hometown of Torrance.

Louis was excited that his hero and role model, Glenn Cunningham, was competing for the 1,500-meter spot that year. While he was sure to show a keen interest in his hero's outcome, his primary focus had to be on the 5,000-meter race that he would be running.

The challenge that he was facing was greatly exacerbated by the heat that day, with the race taking place during the North American heat wave of 1936. The heat was such a factor that many of the participants, including one of the co-favorites, collapsed because of it.

Still, Louis mustered the fighting spirit that he exacted on his bullies and pushed through, leading to a sprint finish at the race's conclusion against Don Lash, who was an American record-holder at the time.

Inexperienced, exhausted, and unfavored. Louis inexplicably forced a dead-heat tie with Lash and qualified for the Olympics at just 19 years and 178 days old, a record that sees him remain as the youngest American 5,000-meter qualifier to this day (*Louis Zamperini*, 2019) and the youngest American runner to make the Olympics team (Hillenbr, 2010).

Louis arrived in Germany on a luxury steamship on July 24, 1936, as part of the Olympic team. Stuffed from the ship's seemingly endless buffet, he was experiencing things he thought were never possible, but what he really wanted to experience was Olympic gold.

Not that he or Lash were given much of a chance: They were facing a Finnish team that had been so dominant in the 5,000 meters that they had won the gold medal in four of the last five Olympic tournaments. Lauri Lehtinen, the defending champion, presented a seemingly insurmountable mountain for Louis to climb.

He barely squeaked out his heat, taking the fifth and final qualifying spot, having struggled under the weight of all of the food that he'd gorged on throughout his travels. Despite struggling, he showed the heart that he would become so synonymous with and was to run in the finals alongside the world's elite.

With only three days to prepare, Louis pushed himself to his limit in the heat of the German summer to give himself the best chance possible. While he wouldn't achieve the improbable win that he dreamt of, Louis would take eighth place in the event that was attended by more than 100,000 spectators.

He finished well ahead of Lash back in thirteenth, but behind the dominant Finns, who would not only win again but would also break more records in the process.

Louis had broken a personal record of his own, though, racing around his final lap in just 56 seconds, with his body at its most tired (*Louis Zamperini*, 2019). The only thing that drove him through his last lap was heart and determination—two attributes that caught the eye of the observing Adolf Hitler, the man who he would soon be fighting tooth and nail to stop.

After somewhat finding his footing and cleaning himself up, Louis climbed into the stands and requested that a member of Hitler's entourage snap a picture of Adolf Hitler for him. The man that he asked was Joseph Goebbels, and after obliging him with the picture, he summoned the exhausted Louis over to speak to Hitler personally.

The two shook hands before Hitler praised Louis for the speed of his final lap via a translator.

I'm sure that day, Louis believed that it would be the last time he would find himself associated with Hitler. In fact, I'm sure that when Louis returned home to a hero's welcome, the only thing on his mind was qualifying for the Olympics in 1940.

However, as we now know, just three short years later, Hitler would commence with Germany's invasion of Poland, and World War II would begin.

The Heroic Act

In September of 1941, with the Americans growing increasingly anxious about the Nazi invasion taking place across Europe, Louis would take the brave decision to enlist in the United States Air Force.

He trained as a bombardier and earned a commission as a second lieutenant before commencing his first post on the Pacific Island of Funafuti on *Superman,* a Consolidated B-24 Liberator bomber.

Louis flew B-24s as part of several successful bombing raids throughout 1943. He caught the attention of the media in April when the *New York Times* named him personally as the man who saved the lives of two fellow soldiers after a successful bombing mission against the Island of Nauru.

After their successful raid, Louis and his craft were attacked by a trio of buzzing Japanese Zeros. The Zeros did significant damage, piercing the bomber's fuselage and tail with a mosaic of 594 bullets and flattening one of its tires.

The attack significantly wounded five crew members and killed one, but the death count would have surely been higher without the prompt first aid that Louis administered.

Following the attack, the *Superman* was no longer airworthy, leading to Louis and his fellow crew members being reassigned to Hawaii. It was after this reassignment that the sheer volume of his bravery and heroism would be truly tested just a month later when he was tasked with embarking on a search and rescue mission for a missing plane.

Before taking flight in May of 1943, Louis focused himself by running a mile in less than 4 minutes and 12 seconds, despite doing so across the sand (*Unbroken: Chapters 10 – 11*, n.d.). The focus and direction that running had once provided his life did so once again, and now it was to prepare him for what would be the toughest test of his life.

While airborne and searching for the missing plane and the crew that were feared to have perished within it, Louis' own B-24 suffered mechanical difficulties and suddenly dropped out of the sky.

The B-24 collided with the Pacific Ocean at such speed that it may as well have been concrete, and the sickening impact took the lives of eight of the 11-man crew instantly. The trio of survivors included Louis, but the odds were far from in their favor. Now, they were stranded in the Pacific Ocean on a couple of rubber life rafts.

After salvaging what they could from the wreckage, including a few tools, they managed to fashion a fishing line. Louis and the two surviving crew members were at the mercy of the elements and severely lacking food and water.

They were forced to eat raw fish and birds that they were fortunate enough to get their hands on and desperately cupped their bloody hands to catch falling rainwater that the heavens were gracious enough to offer them.

The survivors managed to catch two albatrosses and showed restraint by eating only one before killing the other and using its flesh as bait for catching fish.

The trio passed the time by sharing stories about their lives and families and pretending to cook the meals that they missed the most. Sadly, after 33 days of struggle, the trio would become a duo when one of the members died, and Louis and his fellow survivor were forced to wrap his body up and push it overboard.

At that point, it would have been impossible for Louis to resist considering his own fate and fearing that he would be next. Still, the surviving pair fought on in the face of a vicious storm that nearly capsized them. They swatted at sharks with the heavy strikes of a wooden oar and were even peppered by the bullets of strafing Japanese pilots from above. While the airborne attack wasn't able to hit either of the survivors, it riddled their raft with bullet holes and caused such damage that the raft was sagging and struggling to support their ever-dwindling weight. On July 15, after the pair had been adrift for 47 days, they drifted toward the Marshall Islands, where they were immediately accosted by the Japanese Navy.

Although they may have been free from the perilous and choppy waters of the Pacific Ocean, the pair were far from being safe.

After being modestly patched up and nursed back to health, they were immediately transferred to a prisoner of war (POW) camp in Kwajalein Atoll and would be separated.

Louis was then transferred to various POW camps throughout the war.

Japanese POW camps were notoriously cruel, and nearly a third of the Allied POWs died within them (*WWII 75: Marching to Victory*, 2020). Had Japan won the war, their plan was to kill the rest of them too.

Due to his running fame, Louis was treated particularly harshly by the Japanese soldiers. His frail body was constantly on the brink of starvation, and he was forced to weakly shovel coal and clean latrines with whatever energy reserves he could muster. The beatings were as relentless as the cold and damp conditions, and he soon fell ill; he developed beriberi due to a vitamin deficiency.

Despite the torrid time that he suffered, he managed to keep his spirits up. He did his best to distract his fellow prisoners from their plight by writing Italian food recipes and fantasizing about the food that they hoped they would enjoy in the future.

For Louis, though, the future was looking increasingly bleak, and it's far from an exaggeration to say that he was quite literally on the brink of death. In fact, to those back home, he was already considered dead.

He had never been registered as a prisoner of war, so he had been declared first as missing in action and then as killed in action. Even the most hopeful of his friends and family couldn't have expected to see him ever again. Had it not been for the atomic bomb that the United States dropped on Japan on August 6, 1945, they probably wouldn't have.

Less than a month after Hiroshima had been reduced to rubble, the Japanese had surrendered. Then came an influx of Allied planes that dropped food, cigarettes, and the greatest news that could possibly be bestowed on the surviving POWs. One of them was Louis, who mustered all of the determination that he had left to reach the finish line once more.

By the time Louis had regained his health and was released, it had been over two years since his plane fatefully crashed into the Pacific Ocean. In the interim, the United States had awarded a Purple Heart to his parents posthumously, and his friends and family had begun the process of mourning with the town of Torrance.

When Louis finally returned home on October 5, 1945, he was met with a raucous hero's welcome that must have felt far greater than the adulation of the 100,000 spectators who attended the Olympics in 1936.

The Aftermath of the Act

Louis married Cynthia Applewhite in 1946, and the pair had two children. Applewhite died in 2001 but had a profound impact on Louis throughout their marriage and was able to help him calm his mind of the horrific mental scars that his time as a prisoner of war had left him with. Having been plagued with nightmares about strangling his captors following his return home, Louis turned to alcohol to try and ease his mind. Although his body had returned home, his mind hadn't.

With his wife's encouragement, Louis became a born-again Christian and was bold enough to forgive his captors. He even went so far as to visit them and forgive them face-to-face. Only after forgiving those who had inflicted such pain on him was he able to find peace.

When he was just shy of his 81st birthday, Louis ran a leg in the Olympic Torch relay for the Winter Olympics held in Japan in 1998. The Olympics were poignantly held close to where he was once tortured within a prisoner of war camp, a point that wasn't lost on him.

Before heading home, he continued his attempts to spread the message of forgiveness when he requested a meeting with the prison guard who was most brutal to him during his time as a prisoner, but his request was denied.

Undeterred, Louis penned a letter to the guard instead, wherein he stated that he forgave him for the mistreatment that he'd bestowed upon him.

He would sadly never receive notification as to whether his letter was read, but he could rest assured that he'd extended his half of an olive branch that many simply wouldn't have offered.

In 2005, Louis returned to visit Germany and the Olympic Stadium in Berlin, where he'd skyrocketed to fame as a teenager, bringing his journey somewhat full circle. In 2012, he was also invited on the *Tonight Show with Jay Leno,* and his exploits across the Olympics and World War II were celebrated.

It was in 2014 that Louis would reach the finish line of life, passing away after a bout of pneumonia in his Los Angeles home at the age of 97.

A Lasting Legacy

Louis left behind an incredible legacy that has been justly recognized and celebrated. He penned two memoirs to tell large parts of his story, and in 2010, a biography based on his life was released, titled *Unbroken: A World War II Story of Survival, Resilience, and Redemption.* His story resonated so strongly that *Time Magazine* named it the best nonfiction book of 2010 (*The Top 10 of Everything in 2010*, 2010), and it was honored as number one on the *New York Times Bestseller* list (Cowles, 2011).

Two movies have been created that depict his incredible story throughout the war, and a sequel has been made that explores his recovery from his time as a prisoner of war. All of them have titles that are variations on *Unbroken* and adapted from the aforementioned memoirs. A documentary was also released that explored his newfound faith and his path to forgiveness.

Of course, away from the media, Louis has been rightly honored with a plethora of military awards, honors, and citations, including (*Zamperini, Louis Silvie "Louie,"* n.d.):

- Presidential Unit Citation
- Bombardier Badge
- Distinguished Flying Cross
- Air Medal with three oak leaf clusters
- Philippine Liberation Medal with one service star
- American Defense Service Medal
- Asiatic-Pacific Campaign Medal with three service stars

- Purple Heart with one oak leaf cluster
- Prisoner of War Medal
- World War II Victory Medal

His official awards were also supplemented with honors and memorials that will ensure his name lives on. There's a race at Madison Square Garden called the *Louis Zamperini Invitational Mile*. Torrance renamed their airport Zamperini Field, and Torrance High School also renamed both an entrance plaza and their home sports stadium in Zamperini's honor.

In 2008, he was awarded the Ellis Island Medal of Honor and inducted into Chicago's National Italian American Sports Hall of Fame in the same year. Louis was very busy in 2011, throwing the first pitch at a Red Sox game and receiving honorary degrees from both Azusa Pacific and Bryant Universities.

Louis wasn't done, and that same year, he also delivered Bryant University's prestigious baccalaureate address before receiving the school's inaugural Distinguished Character Award.

Louis gave such a moving speech at Magellan Christian Academy's graduation ceremony that he received a 10-minute standing ovation from the 700 attendees. Then, in late July of the same year, he was awarded the Kappa Sigma Golden Heart Award.

In 2015, the United States Air Force Academy named him as the class exemplar for his service and courage.

He also served as the Grand Marshal of the 2016 Rose Parade and was further honored by the tournament after his death. Finally, he had a military dining facility and a 2-mile stretch of the 405-freeway named in his honor.

Louis Zamperini was justly honored by both the public and his military brothers, and hopefully, we've done our part to honor him in this publication, as well.

Chapter 15:

Florence Finch

Spy, the Philippine Islands, 1942-1944

I feel very humble, because my activities in the war effort were trivial compared with those of the people who gave their lives for their country. – Florence Finch

The Background of the Hero

Florence Finch was born Loring May Ebersole on October 11, 1915. She was born in Santiago City of the Philippines at a time when the country was under American colonial rule. Her father was a U.S. Army veteran who had settled in the country after fighting in the Spanish-American War, and her mother was a Filipino native.

When Florence graduated high school, she followed in her father's footsteps and found employment as a civilian stenographer for General Douglas MacArthur's army intelligence unit in Manila.

It was during her time there that she met the man who would become her first husband, Charles Smith, who was serving in the U.S. Army as a Navy PT boatman. The two would marry on August 19, 1941, but like most of the heroes featured throughout this publication, Florence's life was forever changed on December 7, 1941, when the Japanese executed a surprise attack on Pearl Harbor.

While Florence may not have been present at Pearl Harbor, she would soon feel the aftershocks of the devastating attack.

Manila would fall to the Japanese on January 2, 1942, just shy of a month after the U.S. had been dragged into the Second World War by the Japanese. Before Florence had time to assess the chaos that was unfolding around her, her husband was killed in action just a month later.

The pair had only been married for six months. When her husband reported to his boat to bravely re-supply the American and Filipino troops who were trapped on the Bataan Peninsula and Corregidor Island, he was killed in action.

The Japanese had killed her husband and invaded her home, but Florence didn't have the firepower to exact revenge. So, she instead used cunning, patience, and resilience to undermine them from the inside.

The Heroic Act

Florence's greatest asset during that time was her dual citizenship. As an Asian-American, she was able to avoid internment by claiming Philippine citizenship and taking up employment in the Japanese-controlled Philippine Liquid Fuel Distributing Union.

Not at all content with simply evading capture, Florence saw an opportunity in her role that included writing vouchers for the distribution of alcohol, fuel, oil, and diesel. First, she began sabotaging key Japanese shipments by diverting them to the Philippine Underground, a resistance movement striving to help take their country back.

Over time, she became more daring and, unbeknownst to those around her, started organizing the destruction of Japanese supplies. She was unassuming and quiet, the last person the Japanese would imagine was internally gnawing away at their cause.

With the Japanese weakening somewhat, and the Philippine Underground growing in strength thanks to her diversion of supplies, Florence had already played a major part in trying to help her country fight back. At the height of her operations, she was diverting up to 250 gallons of fuel every week by cleverly falsifying records (*Florence Finch*, n.d.).

There was no need for her to take any further risk that would increase the odds of her plan being uncovered. Yet, when her former U.S. Army intelligence boss managed to contact her and reveal the horrendous conditions that the POWs were being kept in, she knew that she would have to step up her efforts even further. Florence began putting a portion of her salary aside so that she could buy food and medicine. Then, with the help of the Philippine Underground, other former employees of the Army intelligence unit that she worked for, and brave civilians, she masterminded the smuggling of it into POW camps via their laundry.

Florence worked diligently to undermine the Japanese and ease the pain of the POWs for three years until she was unearthed and arrested in October 1944. Now, Florence would become a POW herself, and her survival would depend on one thing—resilience.

Following her capture, Florence endured heinous torture at the hands of the Japanese, desperately trying to unearth information on the Philippine Underground. Their torturous efforts included strapping her to a chair and interrogating her as electricity was fired through metal finger clamps.

Even though she was forced through horrendous pain, the Japanese couldn't break her, and when she refused to divulge any information, she was given a sham trial and sentenced to three years of hard labor at Bilibid Prison as a high-value POW.

High-value POWs were placed in cells so small that they had no room to stand and were forced to squat for most of the day. She was fed just one bowl of rice gruel every day and knew that her days were numbered when she started to hear the names of other captives being called for execution.

Still, Florence never divulged a crumb of information or gave a single name over. She was prepared to die for her two countries. Thankfully, she would be spared that fate in February of 1945 when the Americans tore through the Japanese in the Battle of Manila and subsequently liberated the prison camp in which she had been housed. When they found Florence in her tiny, 2 x 4 cell, she had shrunk to just 80 pounds and was surely days from death (Thiesen, 2022).

Following her liberation and transfer to her late father's hometown of Buffalo, Florence was undeterred in her burning desire to avenge her husband's death. On July 13, 1945, she enlisted in the U.S. Coast Guard, joining the Coast Guard Women's Reserve and becoming one of the first Asian-American women to proudly wear the prestigious Coast Guard uniform (Thiesen, 2022).

While she wouldn't see action as a member of the Coast Guard, her willingness to enlist despite everything she endured is a testament to her bravery and loyalty to both her countries.

Aftermath of the Act

Florence was discharged from the Coast Guard in May of 1946 and soon met Robert Finch, a U.S. Army veteran. The pair married and settled in Ithaca, New York, where Florence would spend the rest of her life.

Florence raised a family in Ithaca while working as a secretary at Cornell University. Her community and co-workers had no idea about her incredible feats, which had helped to secure their freedom. She remained humble and happy to move on from the war.

Before Florence passed away at the age of 101 in 2016, her humility shone brightly when she downplayed her efforts and claimed they were "trivial" compared to others who had fought for the country (Thiesen, 2022). Florence was honored with a military funeral and full honors at Ithaca's Pleasant Grove Cemetery in 2017. Incredibly, one of Florence's last wishes was to delay her own burial due to not wanting to disrupt the

Christmas plans of those who wanted to attend her funeral by requiring them to travel through an unforgiving Ithaca winter. It was the Coast Guard's insistence of honoring Florence in this way that ensured her story was illuminated to the country; otherwise, she would have humbly allowed her own story to be lost in history.

A Lasting Legacy

In November of 1947, Florence was awarded the highest honor bestowed on U.S. civilians, the Medal of Freedom, and her citation reads:

> For meritorious service which had aided the United States in the prosecution of the war against the enemy in the Philippine Islands, from June 1942 to February 1945. Upon the Japanese occupation of the Philippine Islands, Mrs. Finch [then Mrs. Florence Ebersole Smith] believing she could be of more assistance outside the prison camp, refused to disclose her United States citizenship. She displayed outstanding courage and marked resourcefulness in providing vitally needed food, medicine, and supplies for American Prisoners of War and internees, and in sabotaging Japanese stocks of critical items . . . .
>
> She constantly risked her life in secretly furnishing money and clothing to American Prisoners of War, and in carrying communications for them. In consequence she was apprehended by the Japanese, tortured, and imprisoned until rescued by American troops. Through her inspiring bravery, resourcefulness, and devotion to the cause of freedom, Mrs. Finch made a distinct contribution to the welfare and morale of American Prisoners of War on Luzon. (Thiesen, 2022)

She was also the first woman to be awarded the Asiatic-Pacific Campaign Ribbon (Finch, n.d.). With Florence living a quiet life, her incredible actions had been mostly forgotten by the rest of the country. That was until the 28th of March in 1995 when the Coast Guard decided to honor Florence's contributions at the opening of a new headquarters on the 50th anniversary of the climax of World War II.

Thus, the $3.5 million headquarters was opened on Sand Island and named in her honor. Determined to ensure her name lived on, in 2019, the Coast Guard then announced that they would be naming a Fast Response Cutter, the *Seaman First Class Florence Finch.*

In the media, Florence was the subject of a book published in 2020. *The Indomitable Florence Finch* was written using a combination of Finch's own first-hand experiences and the diaries of her superiors.

Florence Finch was a survivor who never let go of her beliefs, even in the face of such violence. Her actions were both commendable and inspirational.

Chapter 16:

Charles Thomas

United States Army, France, 1944

Deploy the guns and start firing or we are dead. –Charles Thomas

Background of the Hero

Charles was born in Birmingham, Alabama, on April 17, 1920. He wouldn't spend long in Alabama, though; his family would soon join many other African-American families in moving to Detroit, where the city's black population was growing rapidly.

He showed a very early interest in electronics and planes and graduated from Cass Technical High School in 1938. Following his graduation, Charles joined his father at the Ford River Rouge Factory, where he worked as a steel molder.

The factory was far from the end goal for Charles, and he shortly enrolled at Wayne State University to study mechanical engineering. As we now know, just a couple of years into his studies, America would need soldiers, and Charles was ready to play his part.

He was drafted into the Army in January 1942, and by the time the war reached its earth-shattering conclusion, he had played a major role in the Allies' crucial victory.

Charles started his military career as an infantryman, but his impressive performance during basic and advanced infantry training saw him chosen as an outstanding candidate for officer training school. He was transferred to Camp Wolters in Texas, where he would become a member of one of the U.S.'s newly formed tank destroyer units.

By March 1943, Charles had reported to Camp Carson in Colorado and been assigned to Company C of the 614th Tank Destroyer Battalion.

Like the rest of the African-American heroes within this publication, Charles faced the issues of the racially segregated army, and while he was surrounded by other black soldiers, all of the officers assigned to their unit were white.

At that time, there were also stark differences between the equipment the all-black units had at their disposal and that of the white units. The old and broken equipment that Charles' unit was forced to endure was far less efficient and needed constant repairs, even in the heat of battle, placing them right behind the eight ball before they were even deployed.

I'm sure that Charles and his unit would be forgiven for feeling completely detached from the rest of the Army they were fighting alongside because of the lack of recreational facilities and banishment from the "white" facilities that they faced. Yet, they still laid their lives down for those who were ostracizing them.

Despite the challenges he was confronted with, Charles still managed to impress to such an extent that he earned the rank of sergeant and was selected to attend the Tank Destroyer Officer Candidate School (OCS) at Camp Hood in Texas in December 1942.

When Charles graduated from OCS on March 11, 1943, he did so as a second lieutenant. He returned to his battalion and was then bestowed the honor of assuming command of it, tasked with preparing his men for a move to Camp Hood in Texas.

In August 1944, Charles and the 614th would first deploy to England before traveling to France, where they joined General Patton's Third Army. The 614th was operating as a tow unit at that time, tasking them with using halftracks to tow anti-tank guns into battle. The men tasked with towing the guns were flanked by a small fleet of lightly armored vehicles and a group of infantry soldiers.

It was a dangerous job, but one that needed to be done, and Charles and his men did so valiantly. When Company C of the 614th Tank Destroyer Battalion saw their first action along the French-German border at the end of November, they were fighting alongside the 103rd Infantry Division, and were successful in destroying German observation posts, machine gun nests, and pillboxes. The 614th had arrived, and they were ready to deal serious damage to their German enemies.

The Heroic Act

A month later, on December 14, Charles would lead his battalion into battle and display the act of courage and valor that earned him a rightful berth in this publication.

The U.S. Army needed to capture the French village of Climbach, with it providing a key strategic position just five miles from the German border. However, they had a problem: Very little reconnaissance had been gathered on the village, and the American forces were largely blind to the enemies that were housed within it.

The only way to prevent potentially heavy American casualties was to draw some of the Germans out of the area before the Americans could penetrate the village. They needed a distraction, and Charles was more than willing to thrust his hand high and offer to lead the way and command the platoon from a lead M-20 scout car.

Charles knew of the danger of the mission but was also keenly aware of its importance.

Fearing the village was rife with armored German vehicles, his plan was to draw the first heavy blow toward him, leaving them vulnerable to an American counterattack.

The plan commenced, and Charles led the column from his scout car, knowing that he only had a thin shield of light armor standing between him and potential German artillery, and that it would perhaps be his last mission.

The morning was damp, and there was a thin layer of fog hanging in the air—perhaps Charles hoped that the fog would provide a little feeble cover. Unfortunately, the fog was no ally, and as his scout car crested a rise on the high ground southeast of Climbach, the Germans struck without hesitation or mercy. Artillery and gunfire from 700 yards away tore right through the car's armor and soon disabled it entirely.

Left as a sitting duck, Charles was severely wounded by the onslaught and barely mustered a signal to halt the rest of the column in the cracked rear-view mirror.

He fought his way out of doors that had been welded shut by the impact and rushed around to the front of the vehicle seconds before it was hit by an anti-tank gun. He ordered his brothers from the vehicle in a bid to get them away safely, but machine gun fire promptly tore through his legs, chest, and left arm.

Forced to take cover behind the mangled scout car, despite his wounds and heavy blood loss, Charles defiantly ordered two M-5 anti-tank guns into place and directed torrential fire back at their well-prepared enemy.

The order that Charles was giving the men was one that saw them venture out into the open field and directly into the line of German fire. It was simply the only option they had if they were to return it.

Yet, the gunners were inspired enough by Charles' actions that they deployed their M5 guns with reckless abandon and without hesitation.

As expected, the casualties were vast, as the gunners were greeted with an avalanche of artillery, mortar, small arms, and machine gun fire. The Germans knew that the M5s had the power to unhinge them and were desperate to eliminate them as soon as possible.

On another day, the German firepower might have been enough to force the gunners into retreat. But on that day, with their wounded commander yards from their position, the Americans refused to push back and refused to flinch.

With men falling at a rapid pace and two of the M5s disabled, every man left standing, even those badly wounded, shifted from weapon to weapon and continued laying down heavy fire so that their American brothers could push on to Climbach.

Charles was realistic about his condition and knew that his body couldn't continue to command the platoon the way that his mind wanted to. Thus, he summoned the platoon commander and gave him information on the situation, pinpointing enemy positions and advising on the platoon's ammunition levels.

Despite suffering heavy blood loss, Charles only allowed himself to be evacuated once he was certain that the platoon commander had a firm grasp of things.

The Aftermath of the Act

For the rest of the inspired 614, the battle was far from over. With no idea as to whether or not Charles would survive his wounds, they had to make sure his sacrifice meant something.

The German infantry became so desperate to disable the two remaining guns that they rushed out from the cover of a nearby forest to launch an assault up close and personally. Despite being outgunned and outmanned, the Americans stood tall and refused to retreat an inch.

The Americans left a small arms team in place to continue laying heavy fire down with the M5s, and the rest fanned out so that they could meet the Germans head-on.

The fighting was bloody and fierce, and at one point, an American soldier was forced to mount a half-track that was burning so that he could utilize a 50-caliber machine gun.

The Americans were winning, and the Germans were forced to not just inch back, but to retreat at speed. As the Americans started to run low, brave gunners from Charles' 614 volunteered to rush ammunition 30 yards in the wide open to help restock those at the front of the battle.

Charles and the 614 were a vital cog of the American machine.

Despite enduring more than a 50% casualty rate during the battle (*Charles L. Thomas*, 2024), the 614 were eventually able to help the 103rd Division capture the village of Climbach. While the sheer number of heroes that stood tall that day is impossible to pin down, I feel it's worth mentioning that two of the gunners who nobly took to the open field that day under Charles' direction were rightly awarded posthumous Silver Stars.

As for Charles, he was able to fully recover and continued to serve in the Army for another four years until his well-earned retirement in 1947 with the distinguished rank of major. He would marry his partner in 1949, and the two would have two children. At this time, he also embarked on new careers, first as a missile technician and then as a computer programmer.

When remarking on his actions that day, Charles was typically humble and joked that, "I know I was sent out to locate and draw the enemy fire, but I didn't mean to draw that much." His comrade, Lieutenant Claude Ramsay, was much less understated in his description of Charles' role, proudly proclaiming that the victory and capture of Climbach "belonged" to him and that the bedrock of the victory was the belief that his men had in him (Lengel, 2020).

Charles passed away from cancer on the 15th of February in 1980 and was laid to rest in Westlawn Cemetery in Wayne, Michigan.

A Lasting Legacy

Like the majority of the other African-American heroes honored in this publication, Charles would receive his Medal of Honor posthumously and would never know that he was bestowed the military's highest honor.

He was originally awarded the Distinguished Service Cross in 1945, which was eventually upgraded to a Medal of Honor in 1997. The Medal of Honor was awarded to one of Charles' proud nieces, and his citation reads:

> For conspicuous gallantry and intrepidity at the risk of his life above and beyond the call of duty: Then Lieutenant Charles L. Thomas distinguished himself by extraordinary heroism in action on 14 December 1944. One platoon of Company C, 614th Tank Destroyer Battalion, was designated as the lead element in a task force formed to storm and capture the village of Climbach, France. Lieutenant Thomas, the Commanding Officer of Company C, realized, with the obscurity of information regarding the enemy and a complete lack of reconnaissance, the mission would be an extremely dangerous one.
>
> Fully cognizant of the danger, Lieutenant Thomas volunteered to command the selected platoon of his company and ride in the column's leading vehicle - a highly maneuverable, but equally vulnerable, M-20 scout car. Lieutenant Thomas knew that if there was a concentration of enemy armor in the village, as was believed, he would absorb the initial shock of the first

enemy resistance. The task force left Preuschdorf, France, at 1023 hours, and proceeded to advance in column toward Climbach. Lieutenant Thomas in his scout car stayed well in front of the column. At 1400 hours, upon reaching the high ground southeast of the village, Lieutenant Thomas experienced initial contact with the enemy. As his scout car advanced to an exposed position on the heights, he received intense direct fire from enemy artillery, self-propelled guns, and small arms at a range of seven hundred yards.

The first burst of hostile fire disabled the scout car and severely wounded Lieutenant Thomas. He immediately signaled the column to halt. Before leaving the wrecked vehicle, Lieutenant Thomas and the crew found themselves subjected to a veritable hail of enemy fire. Lieutenant Thomas received multiple gunshot wounds in his chest, legs, and left arm. In spite of the intense pain caused by his wounds, Lieutenant Thomas ordered and directed the dispersion and emplacement of his first two antitank guns. In a few minutes these guns were effectively returning the enemy fire. Realizing that it would be impossible for him to remain in command of the platoon because of his injuries, Lieutenant Thomas then signaled for the platoon commander to join him.

Lieutenant Thomas then thoroughly oriented him as to the enemy gun positions, his ammunition status, and the general situation. Although fully cognizant of the probable drastic consequences of not receiving prompt medical attention, Lieutenant Thomas refused evacuation until he felt certain that his junior officer was in full control of the situation. Only then did Lieutenant Thomas allow his evacuation to the rear. Throughout the action, Lieutenant Thomas displayed magnificent personal courage and a complete disregard

> for his own safety. His extraordinary heroism spurred the soldiers of the platoon to a fierce determination to triumph, and resulted in a mass display of heroism by them. Lieutenant Thomas' intrepid actions throughout the operation reflect the highest traditions of military service. (Thomas, 2024)

He was also awarded the following (Thomas, 2024):

- Combat Infantryman Badge
- Purple Heart
- Army Good Conduct Medal
- American Campaign Medal
- European-African-Middle Eastern Campaign Medal with 3/16" Bronze Star
- World War II Victory Medal

Charles Thomas' selfless actions in providing the necessary distraction for his battalion ensured the vital capture of the village of Climbach. He inspired and empowered men to find strength they didn't feel they had left and is an inspiration to us all.

Chapter 17:

Phil Rasmussen

United States Air Force, Pearl Harbor, 1941

I noticed an aircraft dive down [at] the hangar and pull up very sharply, and an object dropped from this plane. And then I saw this huge orange explosion of smoke and orange flames. And when this airplane pulled up, I saw the two meatballs, or the two round circles identifying it as a Japanese aircraft. I knew immediately that it was a Japanese aircraft. – Phil Rasmussen

Background of the Hero

Phillip Rasmussen was born on May 11, 1918, in Boston, Massachusetts' Suffolk County.

Phil enrolled in flight training in 1940 at the age of 22 and graduated just eight months later. His first assignment was defending against any potential airborne attacks that Wheeler Field on the island of Oahu may face. Despite never being mentioned by name, Phil knew that those attacks were likely to come from the Japanese.

On December 2, 1941, just five days before the now infamous attack on Pearl Harbor, Phil even received a letter from his nervous father, fearing that the Japanese were going to cause the United States trouble.

With his father's words resonating, Phil took to his diary and remarked that he felt the diplomatic efforts of President Franklin D. Roosevelt were failing and that things may soon become serious.

However, he was quick to reassure himself that being 3,000 miles from Japan, it was unlikely that they would target Pearl Harbor—words that he would soon be forced to swallow, along with his fear.

On the day of the Pearl Harbor attack, he was just 23 years old. He had risen to the rank of second lieutenant and was assigned to the 46th Pursuit Squadron at Wheeler Field on the Hawaiian island of Oahu.

Like many soldiers of a similar age at that time, Phil was a young man with only one desire: to fight for his country. On December 7, 1941, he would be given the opportunity to do just that.

The Heroic Act

Still acclimatizing to the sun rising in his eyes, Phil was in the barracks for unmarried officers at the time of the attack, gazing out at the hanger line and taking in the peace of the morning.

He admired rows of American aircraft lined wingtip to wingtip, including P-40s—the best that the Air Force had to offer at the time—and a handful of much older, less technologically advanced P-36s scattered toward the end of the line.

Fatally, the planes had been lined up in such a manner to prevent sabotage from any Japanese sympathizers. Rather than being primed for take-off, the planes were instead packed tightly together, and their ammo was kept well away from them to prevent anyone from quickly loading them up and turning them on American troops.

This, and the fact that the ammunition was stored a fair distance away from the planes themselves, made Phil's actions that day that much more difficult and, therefore, that much more heroic.

As Phil admired the scene, something alarming caught his eye: an aircraft flying low at speed. Before he could even finish his morning coffee, Phil was witnessing a bomb being dropped on his fellow Americans.

They were under attack, and although he instantly recognized the Japanese insignia, the Americans were so ill-prepared that they hadn't even been shown photos of the aircraft that they were being attacked by, making distinguishing the difference between fighter and bomber planes nearly impossible. Phil's instinct took over. He yelled down the hallway to warn his brothers of the attack, sprinted into his room, threw on his shoes, and strapped a webbed belt around his waist before holstering a 45-caliber pistol.

He was soon sprinting toward the flight line in his pajamas, a detail that saw him earn the moniker of "the pajama pilot" (Rasmussen, 2021). When Phil reached the flight line, he was met with a dismal and disturbing sight: Most of the P-40s that he had been admiring that morning were exploding like firecrackers due to the close proximity that they'd lined up in, with each one igniting the next.

He wiped the sweat from his eyes and spotted a glimmer of hope down the opposite end of the line: the trusty, old P-36s—far older and less advanced than the Japanese Zeros that were strafing above him, but just enough to get him into the fight.

Phil proceeded to run the deadliest of gauntlets. With the strafing enemy raining hellfire from above, he moved as quickly as his tired legs would allow him. Thankfully, the enemy above had more pressing targets than one pajama-clad pilot sprinting down the runway, and he was able to reach the P-36s unscathed.

I don't think it's unreasonable to assume that they merely saw Phil as a helpless victim fleeing to safety, but soon, he would take the fight right back to them.

Phil landed in the cockpit of the plane and got it started with force before being joined by a brave armorer, who dragged belts of both 30- and 50-caliber ammunition over his shoulders and jumped onto one of the plane's wings.

Phil taxied the plane to the earthen revetments surrounding the airfield, getting the plane over them. Finding a lull in the bombing, he frantically loaded the plane alongside his armorer.

He soon took to the infested skies, and thankfully, he wasn't the only American who had managed to do so. Flanked by his squadron commander, Lou Sanders, and two other commendable pilots, the four took off in formation and were soon headed toward the chaos at Pearl Harbor.

They climbed steadily, cleverly using the clouds for cover as they clawed for altitude and sought the high ground. As they ascended through the clouds, they took the opportunity to charge their guns with the necessary handle, snapping rounds into the chamber, first the 30-caliber without issue, but then when Phil tried to charge the 50-caliber, he realized that he had a big problem: The 50-caliber gun was broken and would fire at will, forcing him to keep the weapon cocked at all times and giving him another thing to worry about at a time when his brain was already scrambled.

Still, he headed east and was quickly given instructions to head to Bellows Field. However, in the chaos, those instructions were soon pivoted to a new destination—Kaneohe Bay. When they reached Kaneohe Bay, they were met with a catastrophic scene and a bay under heavy and sustained attack.

Met by the sight of eight aircraft mid-turn and preparing another bombardment, Phil and the brave trio alongside him dove toward them, descending as fast as their rickety planes would allow and meeting them at around 6,500 feet.

Phil unknowingly separated from his allies during the descent, meaning he was now all alone. First approached by an attacker from his right side, Phil let fly, releasing the handle on his broken 50-caliber machine gun and leaving it to erratically fire of its own volition.

His bullets pierced the fuselage of his enemy, which soon caught fire, forcing its pilot to peel away in retreat. Phil had no time to revel in his personal victory, as he was quickly forced to evade another attacker who attempted to ram him.

While he was able to use his skill to dodge the attempt, the sharp maneuver was a step too far for his old plane to handle. Already littered with bullets, the canopy of the P-36 that had fought so valiantly for its pilot blew completely off.

The plane was failing on our hero and falling at speed. He desperately wrestled to regain control, working with the control stick and working the trim tabs at a frenetic pace. Finally, he was able to stabilize the juddering craft using every ounce of strength he had left, but he was now without the use of her rudder.

For Phil, it was at this moment that the adrenaline finally started to wane, and the reality of the danger that he had faced hit him like a ton of bricks. He ducked in and out, seeking the desperate reprieve of cover in the clouds, and realized that he'd taken a blow to his head without the protection of a helmet he had no time to grab.

When he reached to check on a potential head wound, he only found shards of plexiglass, revealing that somehow he'd survived the battle without a scratch.

Headed back toward Wheeler Field, Phil was picked up by his commander, Lou Sanders, who pulled up close to him to check on him. He was shaken, but he was okay and assured his commander of that fact before he was escorted back.

Just as it looked like Phil had survived the worst of things, he and his commander suddenly found themselves under fire from panicked Allies at Schofield Barracks, who were simply shooting at anything airborne and had no knowledge that the brave pilots had managed to make it off the ground.

Thankfully, those at Wheeler Field quickly realized that Phil and his commander were friendly, and they were allowed to land safely.

Phil realized that his landing gear had been damaged in the fighting and was forced to desperately pump the emergency hydraulic fluid pump until the gear was released. Wracked in pain and with his muscles burning, Phil cut the plane's engine and landed on the dew-sodden grass below.

Without control of the rudder and no brakes, the plane had a life of its own and landed hard before spinning on the wet grass and finally coming to a natural stop. Finally grounded, Phil sank into the cockpit with relief, sodden with a combination of sweat and residue from the skies that he'd fought so valiantly in.

As men flooded from the hangar line to check on him, Phil dropped from the plane and stared back at his brothers in a daze, incapable of thinking coherently.

Only at this point did Phil realize just how lucky he had been to escape with his life, seeing what was left of the old P-36 that had served just as valiantly as he had: The tail wheel had been shot clean off, the canopy was shattered, and the body of the plane was pierced with more than 500 bullet holes.

He learned that the other pilots who had fought alongside him had done so without functioning weapons and that he could have had a much worse fate than having a gun that would fire on its own.

Perhaps his most startling realization, though, was the fact that the fuselage at the back of his plane had been pierced by a 20-millimeter round, and the only reason he'd survived the explosion was that the plane's radios had absorbed the shockwave.

However, Phil had no time to count his blessings, with ammunition still exploding in the hangers, fires raging around him, and the threat from Japanese planes still hanging from above. He marched into the barracks, peeled his sodden pajamas from his soaked skin, and threw on a flying suit.

For Phil and America, the fight was far from over.

The Aftermath of the Act

After that fateful day, Phil's military career continued, and he had a further impact on World War II, shooting down more Japanese planes and taking part in a key bombing mission over Japan that enabled the Allies to triumph over Axis forces.

Post World War II, he flew in combat missions in the Pacific, Europe, and the Middle East, before his well-earned retirement in 1965 as the Chief of Operations at Eglin AFB.

He lived in Florida after his retirement until he died in 2005, and he was laid to rest in Arlington National Cemetery.

A Lasting Legacy

Phil Rasmussen has left a lasting legacy behind that he and his family can be incredibly proud of. His actions at Pearl Harbor saw him presented with a Silver Star, the citation for which reads:

> The President of the United States of America, authorized by Act of Congress July 9, 1918, takes pleasure in presenting the Silver Star to Second Lieutenant (Air Corps) Philip M. Rasmussen, United States Army Air Forces, for gallantry in action as a Pilot of the 46th Pursuit Squadron, 15th Pursuit Group, at Wheeler Field and over the Island of Oahu, Territory of Hawaii, and waters adjacent thereto, on 7 December 1941.
>
> When surprised by a heavy air attack by Japanese forces on Wheeler Field and vicinity, Second Lieutenant Rasmussen took off for the purpose of attacking the invading forces, without first obtaining information as to the number or type of Japanese in the attacking

> force, and proceeded to patrol in the vicinity of Bellows Field, where he encountered six enemy aircraft. Though outnumbered with only three other aircraft in the flight he immediately attacked the enemy formation and shot one down in flames. He returned his plane safely to Wheeler Field although it had been damaged by enemy machine gun and cannon fire during the encounter.
>
> Lieutenant Rasmussen's presence of mind, coolness under fire against overwhelming odds in his first battle, expert maneuvering of his plane, and determined action contributed to a large extent toward driving off this sudden enemy air attack. (Rasmussen, 2019)

His military achievements also include (Lt Col Philip M. Rasmussen, n.d.):

- Distinguished Flying Cross (that he received for the aforementioned Japanese bombing mission)
- Four Airman's Medals
- American Defense Service Medal
- Army Air Force Pilot Badge
- Asiatic-Pacific Campaign Medal
- World War II Victory Medal

As well as his military accomplishments, Phil was also featured in the movie *Pearl Harbor* and honored with his own memorial in the National Museum of the United States Air Force, depicting him pushing his P-36 in his red and white striped pajamas, and titled, "The Pajama Pilot."

Phil may not have been able to prevent the attack on Pearl Harbor in 1941, but the fact that he knew he couldn't and still took to the skies in the face of insurmountable odds embodies the American spirit that would eventually help the Allies claim victory in World War II.

Chapter 18:

John Basilone

United States Marine Corps, Battle for Henderson Field, 1942

Never fear your enemy but always respect them. –John Basilone

Background of the Hero

John Basilone was born in Buffalo, New York, in 1916. His parents, Salvatore and Theadora, met at a church gathering and had 10 children, of which John was the sixth. Surrounded by siblings, most of whom were bigger and older than him, John had no choice but to toughen up quickly.

John and his family returned to their hometown of Ruritan, New Jersey, in 1918, and it was in Ruritan that he dropped out of middle school at 15. After bouncing around and working as a golf caddy at a local country club, John made the decision to join the military just before his 18th birthday.

He started out as a field cook for the United States Marine Corps and was stationed in various mess halls around the country, preparing meals for the Marines that he hoped he would one day emulate.

It was during this time as a field cook that John's toughness would solidify in front of his military brothers. While stationed in the Philippines, he excelled in the Marine Corps boxing division and became a champion.

In 1937, John returned home from his time serving in the Philippines and started working as a truck driver in the United States. However, he couldn't help but miss the Philippines, so he set about enlisting in the Marine Corps in 1940 in the hopes that he would be sent back there.

John enlisted in Baltimore and was sent for recruit training at the Marine Corps Recruit Depot, Parris Island. From there, he progressed to Marine Corps Bases Quantico and New River. Having graduated with little issues, he was soon stationed at Guantánamo Bay in Cuba.

The Heroic Act

John was assigned to D Company, 1st Battalion, 7th Marines, 1st Marine Division. It was while he was a member of this division that he would perform the first of two heroic acts that saw him earn acclaim.

Having risen to the rank of sergeant in 1942, John found himself locked down during the Battle for Henderson Field on Guadalcanal when his unit was mobbed by a group of roughly 3,000 Japanese soldiers from their Sendai Division, who were armed to the teeth with grenades, machine guns, and mortar.

Comparatively, John and his division were armed with two 30-caliber machine guns. John commanded two machine gun stations by himself with the goal of preventing the Japanese forces from crossing a narrow pass at the Tenaru River.

Outgunned and outmanned, John fought valiantly until he was one of only three Americans left standing.

The Japanese had tactically cut the trio's supply line off from the rear, leaving their ammunition critically low. Knowing that their only choices were finding ammunition, surrendering, or dying, John fought through the Japanese-occupied supply line with just his pistol and a machete.

Once he'd reached the ammunition, he then threw 90 pounds of ammunition and weaponry over his tired shoulders and surged back to his brothers 200 yards away in the machine gun pit while picking off enemies with his Colt .45 pistol in his free hand along the way.

He was then able to not only resupply the weapons but also repair one of them in the heat of battle while firing continuously with the other until reinforcements could reach him. Pinned down, working frantically to repair the broken weapon, and with his finger pinned to the trigger of the other, John showed a sheer will to survive at a time when many would have been waving a reluctant white flag.

With ammunition starting to dwindle once more, John then spent his second day holding off the enemy with just his machete and his pistol, slashing and blasting through them to such an extent that he'd annihilated almost an entire unit on his own.

By the end of the battle, John had been firing a machine gun almost continuously for three days and nights without sleeping, eating, or even taking a moment to rest.

Following the battle, John returned to the United States to take part in war bond tours, and his hometown of Ruritan even threw him a parade! In the eyes of many, he had done more than his part for his country, but the fanfare simply made John uncomfortable, and he longed to get back to helping his brothers.

The Marine Corps denied his first request to return to the front lines and instead offered him an assignment as an instructor, insisting he could continue to help on the home front. It wasn't enough for him, though, and his persistence paid off in 1944 when his request to re-enlist in the Marine Corps was accepted, and he was sent to Camp Pendleton in California for training.

It was while he was stationed in California that he would meet his future wife, Lena Mae Riggi, who was serving as a sergeant in the Marine Corps Women's Reserve. The couple married in 1944 at St. Mary's Star of the Sea Church in California.

Don't be fooled into thinking you're reading the *Aftermath of the Act.* John's acts of heroism were far from over. On February 19, 1945, the invasion of Iwo Jima commenced, and John was front and center as part of C Company, 1st Battalion, 27th Marine Regiment, 5th Marine Division.

He stormed Iwo Jima's red beach with his gunners in tow, but as they trudged up the black sand, they found themselves pinned down by enemy machine gun fire from the heavily fortified blockhouses of the Japanese.

Losing men and unable to progress any further, John rolled his sleeves up and took the long route all the way around the side of the blockhouses. Eventually, his trekking paid off and allowed him to get right above the blockhouse that had his men pinned down.

While evading fire from all angles, he used a combination of grenades and demolitions to single-handedly obliterate the enemy strong point that had prevented his men from progressing, as well as the entire garrison stationed to defend it.

With American troops now free to ascend the Red Beach, John continued his one-man offensive. After fighting his way to Airfield Number 1, he bravely helped to free a Marine tank that was being bombarded with artillery and mortar.

He then inexplicably guided the tank through a minefield despite the mortar and artillery raining down on it, allowing the tank to get back into the fight.

Sadly, after his heroic actions, he was then killed in action. While sources debate whether it was the shrapnel of a mortar shell or a burst of small arms fire striking his left arm, groin, and neck that killed John, what is without debate is that the soldier who took John's life was far too late:

The fallen soldier's actions had already ensured that his brothers were liberated from their landing zone and able to make serious inroads into the Japanese defenses.

The Aftermath of the Act

John was buried at Arlington National Cemetery in Arlington, Virginia. His proud wife Lena would go on to live for another 55 years before passing away at the age of 86 on June 11, 1999.

Lena never remarried and was buried wearing her wedding ring—a true testament to the love that the two shared.

A Lasting Legacy

After his incredibly brave actions, Basilone was the only enlisted Marine to receive both the Medal of Honor and the Navy Cross in 1943.

His Medal of Honor citation reads:

> For extraordinary heroism and conspicuous gallantry in action against enemy Japanese forces, above and beyond the call of duty, while serving with the 1st Battalion, 7th Marines, 1st Marine Division in the Lunga Area, Guadalcanal, Solomon Islands, on 24 and 25 October 1942. While the enemy was hammering at the Marines' defensive positions, Sgt. BASILONE, in charge of 2 sections of heavy machine guns, fought valiantly to check the savage and determined assault. In a fierce frontal attack with the Japanese blasting his guns with grenades and mortar fire, one of Sgt. BASILONE'S sections, with its gun crews, was put out of action, leaving only 2 men able to carry on.
>
> Moving an extra gun into position, he placed it in action, then, under continual fire, repaired another and personally manned it, gallantly holding his line until replacements arrived. A little later, with ammunition critically low and the supply lines cut off, Sgt.

> BASILONE, at great risk of his life and in the face of continued enemy attack, battled his way through hostile lines with urgently needed shells for his gunners, thereby contributing in large measure to the virtual annihilation of a Japanese regiment. His great personal valor and courageous initiative were in keeping with the highest traditions of the U.S. Naval Service. (Medal of Honor Recipients, 2008)

His Navy Cross citation reads:

> For extraordinary heroism while serving as a Leader of a Machine-Gun Section, Company C, 1st Battalion, 27th Marines, 5th Marine Division, in action against enemy Japanese forces on Iwo Jima in the Volcano Islands, 19 February 1945. Shrewdly gauging the tactical situation shortly after landing when his company's advance was held up by the concentrated fire of a heavily fortified Japanese blockhouse, Gunnery Sergeant BASILONE boldly defied the smashing bombardment of heavy caliber fire to work his way around the flank and up to a position directly on top of the blockhouse and then, attacking with grenades and demolitions, single handedly destroyed the entire hostile strong point and its defending garrison.
>
> Consistently daring and aggressive as he fought his way over the battle-torn beach and up the sloping, gun-studded terraces toward Airfield Number 1, he repeatedly exposed himself to the blasting fury of exploding shells and later in the day coolly proceeded to the aid of a friendly tank which had been trapped in an enemy mine field under intense mortar and artillery barrages, skillfully guiding the heavy vehicle over the hazardous terrain to safety, despite the overwhelming volume of hostile fire. In the forefront of the assault at all times, he pushed forward with dauntless courage and

> iron determination until, moving upon the edge of the airfield, he fell, instantly killed by a bursting mortar shell. Stouthearted and indomitable, Gunnery Sergeant BASILONE, by his intrepid initiative, outstanding skill, and valiant spirit of self-sacrifice in the face of the fanatic opposition, contributed materially to the advance of his company during the early critical period of the assault, and his unwavering devotion to duty throughout the bitter conflict was an inspiration to his comrades and reflects the highest credit upon Gunnery Sergeant BASILONE and the United States Naval Service. He gallantly gave his life in the service of his country. (Hoeferlin, 2014)

John would also receive the following awards (John Basilone, 2020):

- Purple Heart
- Marine Corps Good Conduct Medal
- Navy Presidential Unit Citation with one Star
- United States Marine Corps Rifle Sharpshooter Badge
- American Campaign Medal
- Asiatic-Pacific Campaign Medal with two Stars
- American Defense Service Medal with one Star
- World War II Victory Medal

Aside from his incredible military accolades, he was also remembered with a litany of other honors. In 1945, his wife Lena christened a U.S. Navy destroyer named after her husband.

The *USS John Basilone* is a guided missile destroyer that was christened in 2012, and John also has a plaque at the United States Navy Memorial in Washington, D.C.

From entry points and parachute landing zones to the *Basilone Challenge*, which requires recruits to carry concrete-filled ammunition cans up a hill at the Marine Corps Training Depot in San Diego, John's presence is justly felt to this day across the U.S. Military.

He has also been represented in the media, most recently being featured as a major character in the HBO series *The Pacific* (2010).

John Basilone's bravery saved countless American lives and contributed to the Americans' ability to control the Pacific Ocean. His actions should never be forgotten.

Chapter 19:

Jane Kendeigh

United States Naval Nurse, the Battles of Iwo Jima and Okinawa, 1945

Our rewards are wan smiles, a slow nod of appreciation, a gesture, a word—accolades greater, more heart-warming than any medal. –Jane Kendeigh

Background of the Hero

Jane Kendeigh was born in March 1922 and raised in Oberlin, Ohio. She would attend nursing school in Cleveland, from which she would graduate in 1944. It wouldn't be long after her graduation that she became a member of the first class of the Naval School of Air Evacuation.

The goal of the school was to train nurses and doctors in preparation for field survival and crash procedures during combat. The curriculum also focused on treating the wounded at high altitudes, calisthenics, physical conditioning, and aeromedical physiology.

The end goal was the production of a well-equipped team that could rescue and treat wounded soldiers who had been flown out of Okinawa to either San Francisco or Guam.

As you would expect, and as Jane would surely have expected, this brave team was to be dropped right into the heat of battle and thrust onto the front lines to put the lives of others ahead of their own. It was a selfless role, and Jane would prove herself to be exactly the kind of nurse that the role required.

Jane was such an excellent candidate that she was also chosen, along with others who had excelled, to be taught hand-to-hand combat and other skills useful during battle. Upon her graduation in the early months of 1945, she was just 22 years old and already held the distinction of being one of the Navy's first nurses to complete flight training.

She could fly, she could fight, and she could treat wounded soldiers. Jane had all the tools to be a major asset for America, and she certainly would be.

The Heroic Act

Unlike many of the heroes within this publication, Jane's heroic act can't be contained to a particular act or specific action.

After graduation, Jane was originally stationed in Guam. It was at 2:00 a.m. on the morning of March 6, 1945, that she would board a Navy Air Transport Service plane R4D as a member of the Naval Air Transport Service medical evacuation squadron, VRE-1.

She was headed for Iwo Jima, where thousands of stricken American soldiers were in dire need of her help, and she had a Naval photographer in tow who was tasked with capturing pictures of the first Navy nurse in action.

When they arrived at Iwo Jima, the gravity of Jane's situation, and indeed the immediate danger that she was in, became crystal clear. The airfield that they had planned to land within was under heavy attack, and with shells exploding below them like fireworks, her plane circled anxiously and desperately waited for a lull in the carnage so that they could land.

When they were finally able to land, they did so among enemy mortar fire that threatened to clip their wings at any given moment. When Jane shakily descended the ladder, and her feet touched the ground, she immediately made history as the first Naval flight nurse to land in Iwo Jima (Kendeigh, 2020).

She had no time to consider the print she had left on history, however, as the scene she was met with was a chaotic one, and she faced a mammoth task. Met by stricken and bloody soldiers on stretchers, along with what was left of the burning airfield, she set to work quickly and, along with the other nurses, was able to evacuate 16 wounded men. Even in the heat of battle, Jane still faced heckling and wolf whistling from some of the men she was risking her life to save.

Once the plane managed to avoid the mortar shells crashing in from the sky for long enough to take off, the pilot checked on Jane and queried as to whether she had felt scared on the airfield.

She bravely and defiantly told him that she didn't remember being scared and that all she had time for was getting the wounded safely aboard the plane. She did concede, however, that having returned to the plane, her knees had started shaking, and she was struggling to stand, with the adrenaline having then worn off (tara, 2022a).

Her duty was far from finished, and having safely helped treat the 16 wounded en route back to Guam, she spent the next two weeks flying in and out of the war-torn Iwo Jima. Despite facing deadly enemy fire and a constant avalanche of heavy mortar, Jane helped evacuate a total of nearly 2,400 wounded American soldiers.

When she later recalled her deadly trips, she explained that she was simply too busy with her patients to be afraid (*World War II at 75: The Women at Iwo Jima*, 2020).

Their role was key, as the vast speed of their planes meant that they were tasked with rescuing those with the slimmest chance of survival while the others were transported by boat.

In stark contrast to the aggression and violence that she was surrounded by, Jane treated her patients with a gentle touch that restored some humanity in a situation where it had been almost certainly lost.

As quickly as she left her plane, she made mental notes of up to 20 stricken men and got to work. In one specific instance, she fed a wounded soldier who had taken a bullet to the throat through a tube as she comforted him.

When Jane returned home to the United States, she found that her heroics had made her somewhat of a media sensation. After participating in a war bond drive, something was troubling her: She knew that there were more wounded men who needed her help and couldn't simply sit at home.

She soon requested to return to her duties in the Pacific, and on April 7, she landed in Okinawa, becoming the first flight nurse to arrive there, too (*Jane Kendeigh*, 2020). She set to work once more and resumed her rescue mission.

By the time she returned home at the end of the war, she had also served bravely at battlefronts in Hawaii and the Marianas.

Jane and the other flight nurses had treated and rescued a staggering 1,176,048 military patients throughout World War II, and perhaps even more staggering was the fact that only 46 had perished during evacuation (Kendeigh, 2020).

Despite the dangerous environment and lack of sophisticated equipment, Jane and the flight nurses performed miracles.

Aftermath of the Act

After the war, Jane lived in San Diego, California. She passed away on July 19, 1987 at the age of 65 years old.

A Lasting Legacy

Jane's first flight to Iwo Jima was documented by the Naval photographer, who went on to create a scrapbook documenting their journey and supplement the photos with his own handwritten commentary.

The scrapbook serves as a vital piece of Jane's legacy, and its preservation was ensured when it was donated to the National Museum of the Pacific War before being developed into a booklet by the Admiral Nimitz Foundation.

While Jane and the flight nurses would sadly not receive the same recognition as some of the other heroes within this publication, perhaps we can take comfort from the following words from Jane herself: "The wan smile, a slow nod of appreciation, a gesture, a word...were accolades greater, more heart-warming than any medal" (*World War II at 75: The Women at Iwo Jima*, 2020).

Chapter 20:

John R. Fox

United States Army, Sommocolonia, 1944

Fire It! There's more of them than there are of us. Give them hell! –John R. Fox

Background of the Hero

John Fox was born on May 18, 1915. He was the eldest of three children, born in Cincinnati, Ohio, and was raised in rural Wyoming. Having initially enrolled at Ohio State University, John soon transferred to Wilberforce University, where he joined the Reserve Officers Training Corps program.

John was in good company. The program was managed by World War I veteran Captain Aaron R. Fisher at the time. Under Fisher's tutelage, John graduated with an engineering degree on June 13, 1940, and was commissioned as a U.S. Army second lieutenant.

Following his graduation, John was assigned to the all-black Infantry on February 10, 1941, and stationed at Fort Devens in the town of Ayer. It was there that he began his artillery training as part of an antitank unit.

In the late spring of 1941, John's training saw him transferred to Fort Benning in Georgia, then his graduation saw him return to Massachusetts that same year.

John would spend 1942 and the early months of 1943 guarding against German sabotage across New England as a member of the 366th Infantry. This duty was an important one due to the devastation of sabotage attacks that the Germans had managed to inflict during World War I.

In the second half of 1943, John and his unit were transferred to A.P. Hill Reservation in Virginia, and subsequently, Camp Atterbury in Indiana for additional training.

They were eventually stationed in Camp Patrick Henry in Virginia, which is where they were residing on the 27th of March in 1944 when they were dispatched to the European Theater.

John sailed on the *USS General William Mitchell,* initially to Morocco before boarding a train to Algeria. At the end of April, they took to the seas again, but this time they were headed for Naples, Italy.

At the time, Italy was under the tight-fisted rule of the Axis, and it was hoped that the American soldiers could offer some reprieve.

Upon their arrival, the 366th Infantry that John had traveled with was separated into detachments, each of which were assigned different duties. For John, this meant assignment to the 92nd Division in Northern Italy's Po Valley.

It wasn't until early December 1944 that John saw himself attached to the all-black 598th Field Artillery Battalion (FAB), where, under the command of Lieutenant Colonel Robert C. Ross, he performed a truly heroic act that helped ease the Axis' hold on Italy.

The Heroic Act

On December 23, John reported to the war's front lines. Eager to help, he volunteered to take up a four-day observation posting through the Christmas period, in the hilltop village of Sommocolonia.

It was on Christmas Day of 1944 that German troops cunningly and ingeniously snuck into the village, donning civilian clothes, and were quickly able to overrun the unprepared American soldiers within it. The move was an act of brilliance on the Axis' part and forced the Americans to withdraw under an artillery barrage. However, while the majority of his brothers were withdrawing, John stayed put on the second story of a townhouse. He ordered his men to evacuate with the others but opted to stay behind so he could observe German positions and use his insight to report back to the Americans on the village outskirts. It was a brave move and made him invaluable to the rest of the Allies as his vantage point allowed him a clear view of the advancing German soldiers as they converged through the village.

As the Germans advanced through the village and closed in on the vulnerable Allies, John began calling in American artillery strikes that were so close to his own position that he could feel the heat of the shells against his tired face.

They were scoring hits, and John was surely helping slow the Germans' advances.

John's bravery would peak on Boxing Day at approximately 11 a.m., when he called in what would be his last artillery strike. You see, the strike he called in on Boxing Day was called to target his own position. Surrounded by 100 German soldiers, John refuted the hesitation of his brothers and demanded that they reigned fire down on him.

When the Allies' mortar shells crashed through the townhouse that John had been hidden within, they took his life along with a staggering volume of German soldiers.

John's sacrifice had put a stop to German advancement and bought valuable time for the Italian civilians and American soldiers who were desperately retreating. He saved countless lives that day, and it would take just one more week for his brothers to retake the village and relinquish the long-held German control of the area.

Aftermath of the Act

When John's body was eventually recovered, he was found surrounded by the bodies of 100 German soldiers. His remains were returned to his wife, and he was eventually laid to rest in Colebrook Cemetery, Massachusetts.

A Lasting Legacy

Having been initially posthumously awarded the Distinguished Service Cross, John saw his award posthumously upgraded to a Medal of Honor in 1997 after the investigation into racial disparity. The medal was awarded to his widow, and his citation reads:

> For conspicuous gallantry and intrepidity at the risk of his life above and beyond the call of duty: First Lieutenant John R. Fox distinguished himself by extraordinary heroism at the risk of his own life on 26 December 1944 in the Serchio River Valley Sector, in the vicinity of Sommocolonia, Italy. Lieutenant Fox was a member of Cannon Company, 366th Infantry, 92d Infantry Division, acting as a forward observer, while attached to the 598th Field Artillery Battalion.
>
> Christmas Day in the Serchio Valley was spent in positions which had been occupied for some weeks. During Christmas night, there was a gradual influx of enemy soldiers in civilian clothes and by early morning the town was largely in enemy hands. An organized attack by uniformed German formations was launched around 0400 hours, 26 December 1944.
>
> Reports were received that the area was being heavily shelled by everything the Germans had, and although most of the U.S. infantry forces withdrew from the town, Lieutenant Fox and members of his observer party remained behind on the second floor of a house, directing defensive fires. Lieutenant Fox reported at 0800 hours that the Germans were in the streets and

> attacking in strength. He called for artillery fire increasingly close to his own position. He told his battalion commander, "That was just where I wanted it. Bring it in 60 yards!" His commander protested that there was a heavy barrage in the area and the bombardment would be too close.
>
> Lieutenant Fox gave his adjustment, requesting that the barrage be fired. The distance was cut in half. The Germans continued to press forward in large numbers, surrounding the position. Lieutenant Fox again called for artillery fire with the commander protesting again, stating, "Fox, that will be on you!" The last communication from Lieutenant Fox was, "Fire It! There's more of them than there are of us. Give them hell!" The bodies of Lieutenant Fox and his party were found in the vicinity of his position when his position was taken.
>
> This action, by Lieutenant Fox, at the cost of his own life, inflicted heavy casualties, causing the deaths of approximately 100 German soldiers, thereby delaying the advance of the enemy until infantry and artillery units could by reorganized to meet the attack. Lieutenant Fox's extraordinarily valorous actions exemplify the highest traditions of the military service. (Fox, 2019)

John's Medal of Honor was supplemented by the following (John R. Fox Facts for Kids, n.d.):

- Combat Infantryman Badge
- Purple Heart
- Bronze Star Medal

- American Defense Service Medal
- American Campaign Medal
- European-African-Middle Eastern Theater Medal with two 3/16" Bronze Stars
- World War II Victory Medal

John has been honored further by a monument in Sommocolonia that features the eight Italian soldiers who were killed in the artillery barrage along with John. Sommocolonia also dedicated a peace park to John and his unit in 2000.

In 2005, John was immortalized as a 12-inch action figure by Hasbro's *G.I. Joe Medal-of-Honor series.*

An American legion post in John's hometown of Cincinnati, Ohio, is also named after him.

One can only imagine what was racing through John Fox's mind as he called the strike in on his position. His decision is one that most of us can't even fathom, and he should be remembered as a man who disregarded his own life to ensure the eventual Allies' victory.

Chapter 21:

Mildred Fish-Harnack

This image has been used with the kind permission of Eric Carlson.

Freedom Fighter, Germany, 1939–1942

And I, too, so loved Germany. –Mildred Harnack

Background of the Hero

Born Mildred Elizabeth Fish on September 16, 1902, Mildred was raised in Milwaukee, Wisconsin, by a father who bounced between employment as a butcher, horse trader, and insurance salesman. Her mother was a typist and self-taught stenographer. The pair had four children, with Mildred having an older sister and twin siblings.

Mildred enrolled at Milwaukee High School of the Arts (called West Division High School at the time); however, the traumatic death of her father prompted her mother to move Mildred and the twins to live with their older sister in Chevy Chase, Maryland.

The trauma of her father's death, moving across the country, and even watching her mother struggle with the hyperinflation of the 1920s did nothing to knock Mildred's prospects. She attended Western High School in her senior year and integrated herself into her surroundings seamlessly by playing on the baseball and basketball teams, performing in a senior class play, and taking up a role as an editor for the school newspaper.

Following her high school graduation, she was on the move again. First, she studied for two years at George Washington University, and then in 1921, she enrolled at the University of Wisconsin.

Mildred initially tried to progress down the journalism route, working for the *Wisconsin State Journal* as a drama and film critic to support herself financially in her first year of study. Unfortunately, while living in a rooming house that was popular with writers and journalists, she faced gender prejudice from her fellow students. The prejudice she faced prompted her to make a change. Initially majoring in journalism, she switched to humanities before settling on a major in English Literature.

In 1922, Mildred engineered her biggest break to that point in her career when she earned a role as a staff writer for the *Wisconsin Literary Magazine.*

She excelled in her studies, and in 1925, she was awarded a Bachelor of Arts in Humanities. Rather than graduate and ride off into the sunset, Mildred stayed to continue her studies and was awarded a Master of Arts in English just two months later.

Her time at the University of Wisconsin was extremely formative, not just because of her studies. It was during her time there that she met Arvid Harnack, a student from Germany, with whom she would fall in love and who would play a huge role in her future heroics.

Throughout her studies, Mildred was also hugely influenced by William Ellery Leonard, a professor who guided her during the writing of her senior thesis. It was the influence and intense scrutiny of Professor Leonard that helped shape her non-conformist world views.

Shortly after the pair graduated, Mildred and Arvid married at a ceremony held at her brother's farm in Wisconsin. Mildred was so proud of her family name that she insisted on hyphenating the pair's surnames rather than simply taking Arvid's. The Fish-Harnacks were planning their next move, as all graduates do, but would soon be separated when Arvid returned to Germany in 1928.

Mildred then spent a year teaching American literature and English at Goucher College in Baltimore before the distance between herself and her husband became too much to bear, and she decided to join him in Germany.

Her first year in Germany was spent living with Arvid's family, and it wouldn't be long before Germany recognized Mildred's talents the same way that America had previously. That very year, she was awarded a grant that allowed her to work on her doctorate in American literature, which she did at the University of Giessen after a brief stint at the University of Jena. The year was 1929, and despite the imperious rise of the Nazis being four short years away, their presence and influence was keenly felt. Throughout Mildred's studies at the University of Giessen, over half of the student population showed vocal support in favor of the Nazis. The tide was turning, and Mildred, like so many others, was powerless to stop it.

Despite the rising tension throughout Germany at the time, Mildred was undeterred in her desire to learn. Her next move saw her enroll at the University of Berlin in 1931 with financial aid from the Alexander von Humboldt Foundation. She started working as an assistant lecturer in English and American literature, then became a lecturer in her own right. She was so beloved by her students that she managed to triple the course enrollment numbers in just three semesters at the University.

Throughout this time, she was never far from her American roots as a member of Berlin's American expatriate community. From attending dances at the American Student Association to serving as the president of the American Women's Club in Bellevuestraße, she never forgot her beloved country of birth and was a proud American woman.

While in Berlin, Mildred knew the writing was on the wall as she watched the German republic unravel before her eyes. Seeking a solution to the rampant poverty and unemployment that the Great Depression bestowed upon her new home, both Mildred and her family turned toward communism and the Soviet Union.

She was clinging to the hope that the Soviet Union's new five-year plan could provide more work across the country. She was then further empowered by her husband Arvid's establishment of a group of academics who met every month to discuss the planned Soviet economy.

In 1932, Mildred lost her job as a professor in Berlin, thanks to the return of Friedrich Schonemann, a staunch Nazi who had been on leave in the United States. The outreach that Mildred had tried to offer her vulnerable students was now cut, leaving many of them to be sucked in by Nazi propaganda.

Next, the funding that Mildred had been afforded to teach at the Friedrich-Wilhelm University was cut, and her family was forced to move home because of the increasing Nazi presence in the area.

Without employment and being forced to uproot her life again, no one would have blamed Mildred for boarding a boat and heading home to America. While that may have been an option that would have ensured her own safety, it would have also seen her separated from her beloved husband, Arvid.

She made the decision to stay with and to fight, inspire, and educate alongside Arvid.

The Heroic Act

On January 30, 1933, Hitler was appointed as the Chancellor of Germany, and the need for people like Mildred and Arvid was suddenly at an all-time high. Seemingly overnight, Germany had slipped from a parliamentary democracy into a fascist dictatorship.

By the time Hitler was appointed, Mildred had already been hosting secret meetings in her apartment with like-minded thinkers who sought to spread a message to combat that of the Nazis. Mildred was tactful in her quest to add new recruits, vetting them by first inviting them under the guise that their group was, in fact, Nazis before the conversation would reveal the potential recruits' true beliefs.

Her background in education had also equipped Mildred to educate the group, and she would lend them books to help them further their understanding of Hitler's plans.

The group was diverse and made up of Social Democrats, Communists, Jews, Catholics, Atheists, Protestants, and Anarchists. Despite sharing different belief systems and coming from different walks of life, they shared one thing in common—they opposed Hitler's fascist regime.

The group, dubbed *The Circle,* first began writing pamphlets in opposition to Hitler that urged Germans to oppose the Nazis and join the resistance. When Germany began banning radio broadcasts from outside the country, Mildred began translating them to ensure that broadcasts from the likes of British Prime Minister Neville Chamberlain and American President Franklin D. Roosevelt weren't lost on the German public.

At the time, Chamberlain and Roosevelt were seeking to offer opposition to the Nazi propaganda that was being presented to the German public. Mildred was vital in ensuring that their attempts to criticize and expose the Nazi regime penetrated German borders.

By the middle of the 1930s, with Germany closing in on their invasion of Poland and the Nazi presence overwhelming the country, Mildred knew that their already-dangerous efforts would need to be stepped up.

Bear in mind that Mildred and *The Circle* were already walking the most dangerous of tightropes and that anyone caught with one of their leaflets would face prison or incarceration in one of the Nazi's cruel concentration camps.

Taking greater risks may seem reckless, but Mildred could see the writing on the wall, and the Nazi's desire to outgrow German territory was becoming inevitable.

In 1938, with Hitler's invasion of Poland right around the corner, Mildred utilized a connection that she had made while serving as the president of the American Women's Club in Bellevuestraße a year prior. Louise Heath, who was the wife of Donald, the First Secretary and monetary attaché at the U.S. Embassy, would provide Mildred a crucial connection to her American allies as Hitler lit the torch of World War II.

Under the guise of tutoring their son twice a week, Mildred would slip messages into her student's knapsack, which he would then take to his father at the embassy. Mildred conducted this dangerous espionage for two years and would even meet with Donald in the German countryside to exchange intelligence.

While she was in constant communication with the U.S. embassy, her husband, Arvid, was engaging in espionage of his own. Arvid had connections to the Soviet Union and undertook a job at the Ministry of Economics under the guise of being a loyal Nazi so that he could gather intel and undermine Hitler's operations.

Working alongside other resistance groups, Mildred and Arvid were able to orchestrate the escape of Jews from the country. As their influence grew, with *The Circle* growing to become the biggest resistance group in Berlin, they started to plot plans of sabotage against the German government.

As one might expect, the greater influence that Mildred's operation had, the more her paranoia grew. The once defiant symbol of freedom and hope was shrinking to a nervous figure who feared Hitler's Gestapo at every turn.

Sadly, her paranoia proved to be well-founded.

Unbeknownst to Mildred and *The Circle,* the Gestapo had intercepted messages between the defiant group and the Soviet Union in 1941 and had eventually deciphered the addresses of key members of the group. After the news of one of their close friends' arrest, Mildred and Arvid fled Germany, reaching the seaside village of Preila in Nazi-occupied Lithuania. Sadly, before they could complete their daring escape, they were tracked down and arrested.

Aftermath of the Act

The Gestapo's operation had been a major success and had seen them capture 119 members of *The Circle.* Mildred and Arvid were among the group that were shackled and dragged to the basement prison of Gestapo headquarters.

After her arrest, Mildred was to be tried as a traitor.

Before her trial, however, she was to be subjected to horrific torture and interrogation. Many of her imprisoned peers committed suicide so that they could avoid the abuse, but Mildred chose to use her time imprisoned to reconnect with the literature that gave her such joy, translating *Bequest* by Johann Wolfgang von Goethe.

After refusing to give any information throughout her brutal torture, Mildred then stood trial in front of a jury of five Nazis. She was unsurprisingly found guilty and initially sentenced to six years in a hard labor camp.

When Hitler caught wind of Mildred's sentence, already enraged by his defeat in Stalingrad, he demanded that Mildred face execution by beheading instead.

Mildred remained staunch, defiant, and brave as she was transported to Plötzensee's notorious execution center. She met her demise at the blade of a guillotine on February 16, 1943, and was the only American executed on Hitler's direct orders.

Arvid was also sentenced to death by hanging.

Following her execution, her remains were buried in Berlin's Zehlendorf Cemetery, making her the only member of Berlin's anti-fascists with a known burial site.

A Lasting Legacy

Despite her heroism and bravery, Mildred's legacy was initially tainted.

First, the U.S. government concealed information surrounding her story and refused to pursue the possibility of her beheading being a war crime since she had acted as a spy and had received a "fair" trial.

Then, despite her actions being lauded by the United States, and with the country having benefited from her intelligence, her country of birth sought to quietly dismiss Mildred's actions due to persistent claims from the Nazis that she was a spy for the Soviet Union.

As we are all now aware, Mildred and Arvid shared intelligence with both the Soviet Union and America. The pair were sadly still branded as communists instead of being revered as the brave heroes who stood and fought back against Hitler's oppression.

The brush that Mildred was tarred with even led to her family burning many of the letters that she had penned throughout World War II, and that could have been used to further tell her story. It could be surmised that Mildred's story may have been forgotten entirely had it not been for the Nazi War Crimes Disclosure being passed by U.S. Congress in 1998, which led to the declassification of documents that had previously been top secret.

Found within these documents was correspondence between an American intelligence officer who branded Mildred "an American hero" who deserved "honoring," only for his superior to demand her case be buried (Roos, 2023).

In 2021, Mildred's story was told through her surviving letters by Rebecca Donner, her great-great niece, who published *All the Frequent Troubles of Our Days.* Incredibly, while Rebecca was conducting research for her writing of the book, she was able to make contact with Don Heath—the child that Mildred was tutoring while sending messages back and forth in his knapsack! Following a lengthy interview and having handed over wads of letters, diaries, and documents, Don claimed he was now free to die, and he subsequently passed away just a month later (Roos, 2023).

When remarking on the actions of her great-great aunt, Rebecca proudly explained that she taught us how important it is to fight for what you believe in, even if your beliefs are unpopular (Roos, 2023).

Today, Mildred is finally recognized as the American hero that she deserves to be.

There is a cenotaph dedicated to her and Arvid in Berlin's Zehlendorf cemetery, and also a school named in Mildred's honor in the same city. There is a neighborhood in Berlin that was renamed after Mildred, and in 2013, the U.S. ambassador was present as Stolpersteins were laid outside their old home in Berlin where they held their secret meetings with *The Circle.*

In America, Mildred Fish Harnack Day is observed on September 16 in Wisconsin state schools. Milwaukee is home to a public school complex named in honor of Mildred, and there is a sculpture dedicated to her in Madison's Marshall Park in Wisconsin.

The University of Wisconsin-Madison also hosts an annual Human Rights and Democracy Lecture in Mildred's memory. Mildred showed incredible guile and bravery to undermine the Nazi's regime from behind enemy lines, and sadly, paid the ultimate price for doing so.

Chapter 22:

Nicholas Minue

United States Army, Tunisian Campaign, 1943

The courage, fearlessness and aggressiveness displayed by Pvt. Minue in the face of inevitable death was unquestionably the factor that gave his company the offensive spirit that was necessary for advancing and driving the enemy from the entire sector. –President Franklin D. Roosevelt

Background of the Hero

Nicholas Minue was born on Christmas Day of 1900 in Sedden, Poland. His parents, John and Mary, were Ukrainian and soon moved their young family back to their homeland. However, by 1906, Nicholas had moved to New Jersey in the United States, where he was raised alongside his sister and two brothers.

Nicholas only attended school through to the 5th grade before he left to learn the ropes at an engineering firm. At a young age, he was drawn to the heroism of serving his country and initially enlisted in the Army in 1918 so that he could fight in World War I.

Nicholas fought for a year before being discharged, then returned home and became a U.S. citizen, possibly inspired by the fighting he'd done for the country he'd grown to love.

It was in 1927 that Nicholas would re-enlist in the Army, and he remained as a private until a promotion to sergeant was bestowed upon him in the early 1940s. Despite the honor that the promotion brought Nicholas and his family, it also posed him with a conundrum.

Sergeants were seen as valued members of the military tasked with planning and the tactical side of battles, but Nicholas was desperate to fight. He was so desperate, in fact, that he voluntarily gave up his rank and instead accepted the lower rank of private so that he could join his fellow Americans in the trenches.

He got his wish in November of 1942 when he was one of the first soldiers to deploy in the North African theater as a member of Company A of the 6th Armored Infantry Regiment, 1st Armored Division (Lange, 2022).

Nicholas was soon sent to Casablanca as a part of Operation Torch, and he fought his way from Morocco through to Algeria throughout the spring of 1943.

The Heroic Act

On April 28, 1943, Nicholas committed to the heroic act befitting his inclusion in this book—a heroic action that required him to lay down his own life for the benefit of millions.

When Company A and Nicholas found themselves near the Tunisian town of Medjez-el-Bab, which was 50 minutes southwest of what was a critical position on the Axis perimeter, their task was to disable an enemy defensive position along a river valley.

Despite the enemy enjoying the high ground, Company A continued to steadily advance toward the town of Medjez-el-Bab until they were flanked by enemy machine guns that cut their men down to shreds and put them in grave danger of not reaching their target.

Nicholas quickly spotted the source of the attacks and charged toward the enemies' position, armed with his fixed bayonet. He went alone in what was far from a planned attack, thrusting his weapon forward with vigor and aggression in the face of overwhelming odds.

He first burst into enemy entrenchments, slicing his way through 10 men with his bayonet and destroying the machine gun nest that was cutting through his brothers. Then, he moved on to the riflemen entrenched in nearby dugouts, taking more Axis lives. With every step that Nicholas took, he was allowing collective steps to be taken toward their goal by the rest of Company A.

One of the hundreds of shells fired toward Nicholas would eventually halt his advance, wounding him fatally. He continued to fight despite his injuries, and by the time he had drawn his last breath on April 28th, 1943, he had left his mark and ensured that the Allies took a monumental step forward that day.

The Aftermath of the Act

Nicholas' fearless assault sparked inspiration in his comrades and led to a breakthrough in the area that would see the Axis' resistance collapse within just two weeks.

Nicholas was laid to rest in the North Africa American Cemetery and Memorial in the Tunisian suburb of Carthage.

A Lasting Legacy

On April 1, 1944, Nicholas Minue was posthumously awarded the Medal of Honor, becoming the first Ukrainian American to be bestowed with the honor. His citation reads as follows:

> For distinguishing himself conspicuously by gallantry and intrepidity at the loss of his life above and beyond the call of duty in action with the enemy on 28 April 1943, in the vicinity of Majaz al Bab, Tunisia. When the advance of the assault elements of Company A was held up by flanking fire from an enemy machinegun nest, Pvt. Minue voluntarily, alone, and unhesitatingly, with complete disregard of his own welfare, charged the enemy entrenched position with fixed bayonet. Pvt. Minue assaulted the enemy under a withering machinegun and rifle fire, killing approximately 10 enemy machinegunners and riflemen. After completely destroying this position, Pvt. Minue continued forward,

> routing enemy riflemen from dugout positions until he was fatally wounded. The courage, fearlessness and aggressiveness displayed by Pvt. Minue in the face of inevitable death was unquestionably the factor that gave his company the offensive spirit that was necessary for advancing and driving the enemy from the entire sector. (Stories of Sacrifice, n.d.)

Nicholas was also honored with the following awards (Minue, 2024):

- Bronze Star Medal
- Purple Heart
- Good Conduct Medal
- American Campaign Medal
- European-African-Middle Eastern Campaign Medal
- Combat Infantryman Medal
- World War II Victory Medal

Along with his military accomplishments, Nicholas also had a handful of personal honors bestowed upon him, too. These include a vehicle ferry named the *Private Nicholas Minue* that the U.S. Army used between 1956 and 1996, an elementary school in New Jersey, an alleyway and a road in Texas, and sections of U.S. Army operating bases and landing posts dedicated to Nicholas. Nicholas volunteered to fight overseas in World War II despite his rank allowing him reprieve, just as he volunteered to rush the trenches when his brothers were pinned down. He never shirked responsibility or left it to others and is a true American hero.

Chapter 23:

Douglas Munro

United States Coast Guard, Guadalcanal Campaign, 1942

Did they get off? –Douglas Munro

Background of the Hero

Douglas Munro was born to James and Edith in 1919 in Vancouver, Canada. His father had lived in Canada after his own mother, Douglas' grandmother, moved there to remarry the man who would bestow the Munro name upon him. Douglas' own mother, Edith, was born in Liverpool, England. Her family relocated to Canada when she was a child, and the pair married in 1914 at Vancouver's Christ Church Cathedral.

Five years later, Douglas was born, but he spent just two years of his childhood in Canada before his family moved to the city of Cle Elum in Washington, where he would grow up.

Douglas was a talented kid. He showed early talent in both the physical rigor of athletics and sports and had the precision and patience to learn several musical instruments. He learned the harmonica and trumpet and mastered percussion at such a level that he was named the drillmaster of the Sons of the American Legion Drum and Bugle Corps.

While in high school, Douglas joined the local Boy Scout troop and started to impress as a member of the school's wrestling team. He excelled on all fronts and had become a student that his parents could be justly proud of.

Following his high school graduation, he made the decision to enroll in a college close to home, Central Washington College of Education, so that he could fulfill his commitment to the Sons of the American Legion. While studying at college, the accolades kept coming for Douglas when he earned a spot as a male cheerleader.

It would be easy to link the physical accolades outlined above to his future act of heroism, and I don't doubt they played a part.

However, he displayed two much more prevalent traits throughout his childhood: the ability to empathize and to sacrifice.

Unlike most families, the Munro's weren't affected by the Great Depression, which actually put Douglas in a somewhat privileged position. Rather than enjoying the privilege afforded to him, the young man sought to help others. He would collect wood with friends, split the load in half, and then deliver their haul to families that weren't able to heat their homes.

Douglas was an empathetic and caring child, even at an age where he would have been forgiven for not yet being so.

While he was excelling at college, he couldn't help but feel concerned by the ever-worsening situation in Europe and the increasingly dangerous power of Nazi Germany. With an aptitude for helping others, he made the decision to leave college behind and enlist as a member of the U.S. Coast Guard—he wanted to save lives.

His frame was so small that he spent the weeks prior to his induction shoveling food down in a bid to make their minimum weight limit. On the 18th of September, he would fulfill his goal of enlisting as an apprentice seaman. It was also on that day that he'd meet Ray Evans, a fellow recruit that he would soon become so inseparable from that the pair would be dubbed the "the Gold Dust Twins" by their future shipmates (Evans, n.d.).

Douglas underwent recruit training at the Coast Guard Air Station Port Angeles, but at that time, no one was really sure what Coast Guard training looked like. The new recruits spent three days completing a variety of tasks, such as mowing grass, peeling potatoes, and helping with some boat maintenance. Whatever was asked of them, Douglas excelled at, making it no surprise when he was selected as part of the crew on the

USCGC Spencer. It was aboard the *Spencer* that he would be learning on the job while at sea. He was first sent to participate in Neutrality Patrols in the Atlantic Ocean, and the 5,400-mile journey provided ample opportunity for him to graduate to the role of quartermaster. In his new role, he was taught about navigation, log keeping, and maintaining the ship's deck equipment.

Douglas excelled again and soon aimed even higher, with the role of signalman next in his sights. Alongside his friend Evans, every spare moment that Douglas had was spent mastering Morse code, the use of signal flags, and the encoding and decoding of messages. In September 1940, Douglas had achieved his goal and advanced to signalman third class.

He wasn't finished, and soon, he and Evans were volunteering to train as coxswains for landing craft due to a staff shortage. Despite having little to no experience handling small boats, Douglas spent his summer training and appeared to be a natural on the water. Both Douglas and Evans quickly passed their small boat training and were assigned to Transport Division 17. There, they moved between transport ships and trained for what was increasingly looking like United States involvement in World War II.

In December of 1941, the United States officially entered the war, and Douglas believed that he would soon join the action.

The Heroic Act

He was right.

In July of 1942, Douglas was transferred to the *USS McCawley* and headed for the Pacific Ocean to help the fight against the Japanese, who were dominating the area one island at a time.

Being cross trained as both a coxswain and signalman, Douglas was undoubtedly an asset. His first assignment involved using his skills to ferry Marines onto the island of Tulagi. After several successful trips, his next assignment required his skills as a signalman.

Douglas settled into a station on Tulagi's beach and spent the night communicating with Marines using a combination of semaphore flags and blinker lights. This communication provided a key link between the Marines fighting on the island and those on the ships in the Pacific Ocean.

After communicating throughout the night with explosions cracking and illuminating the horizon ahead of him, Douglas had little time for rest the next morning and set to work evacuating as many casualties back to the *McCawley* as his small boat would allow.

As he cut the sagging boat through the water, I'm sure he was in no doubt that he had now joined the war.

Once he'd triumphantly returned the wounded men to the *McCawley,* he volunteered for his next assignment: transferal to a Naval Operating Base (NOB) on the northern coast of Guadalcanal.

The NOB, codenamed *Cactus* (meaning Guadalcanal), was erected at Lunga Point on the Solomon Islands, and its purpose was to provide key communication between forces across land and sea.

While serving at *Cactus,* Douglas was reunited with his best friend, Evans. The two shared a makeshift shack no bigger than 80 square feet that they made themselves out of packing boxes and scrap (J. W. Hurlbut, personal communication, October 2, 1942).

Throughout August and September, Douglas and Evans worked hard to support their brothers, transporting crucial supplies such as ammunition, weapons, and medical supplies, rescuing downed airmen, and collecting casualties to return them to the relative safety of the ships.

On September 20, his selflessness came to the fore once more when he volunteered to lead a search-and-rescue mission via boat. He led the search for a Navy airplane crew that had been shot down over Savo Island. While he wasn't able to recover the crew, he was able to help decipher their location, and they were eventually rescued by a flying boat. Douglas used his sailing prowess to ensure that his own crew returned to the base with only minor injuries despite coming under heavy fire from Japanese soldiers.

The American efforts were paying off, but Japanese forces tactically withdrew to the west side of the river in an attempt to close in on American lines. This withdrawal made the insertion of marine forces necessary, but that insertion wouldn't come without cost.

On September 23, Lieutenant Colonel Lewis Puller led his 1st Battalion, 7th Marines, to the river's west side for an exploratory mission. They were quickly overrun and needed backup. Reinforcement arrived just two days later, with more Marines flocking to join the fight.

However, a worrying message was received by headquarters two days later that was hard to decipher: The assumption was made that Americans were pinned down in firefights across the river. Three companies of 1st Battalion, 7th Marines would join the fight via a beach west of Point Cruz to the rear of the Japanese. Douglas was entrusted with the vital job of getting them there. He was put in charge of two landing craft and eight Higgins boats. His job was to ensure that the Marines were dispatched safely to their designated landing points.

Once the *USS Monssen* had cleared the shore of the enemy with a thunderous bombardment, Douglas led the boats in, safely beaching the Marines on a small reef around 100 yards from their target and started progressing inland.

As ordered, Douglas then withdrew the boats back to Lunga Point along with any casualties they had managed to rescue. The crews were still in the process of refueling their landing craft when they received word that the Marines they had just transported were in trouble and needed immediate evacuation.

The Marines that Douglas had escorted had come under fire from a clever Japanese counteroffensive and been surrounded on a hill. Despite the best efforts of those manning the monstrous *Monssen's* 5-inch caliber guns to create a corridor to the beach, getting there was going to be a tall order for the outmanned Marines.

When asked if Douglas was ready to extract the Marines, he let out a defiant, "Hell, yeah!" before leading his crew back toward the drop-off point as fast as his boat would allow (*Signalman First Class Douglas A. Munro's Medal of Honor*, 2020).

This was to be Douglas' final and finest hour.

The bullets piercing the sides of their boats upon arrival at the rendezvous point made it clear to Douglas and his men that rescue was going to be nearly impossible. Despite being advised to fall back, he pressed forward and slid around to position himself parallel to the shore, putting himself right in the line of fire and refusing to leave the stricken Marines.

His beloved friend Evans provided covering fire with a rattling .30-caliber machine gun while Douglas helped as many Marines as he could into the limited shelter that his boat could offer. Despite the bullets whistling past him, our hero's only focus was the bloody Marines swimming toward him.

With the last marine reaching Douglas' boat, the mission appeared to be successful. But before he could return to Lunga Point, something caught his eye—a landing craft was stuck on a reef and taking heavy fire.

Without any care for his own well-being, Douglas pulled his boat to a stop in a swirl of bloody water and heavy smoke right in front of the vulnerable craft, positioning himself as a human shield between Japanese fire and his brothers.

Douglas and Evans fired their .30 calibers alongside each other, brothers in arms and brothers in life. Their fire provided enough cover for the Marines to free the landing craft and save the lives of those onboard.

The act would require the life of Douglas, though, when shortly after he'd helped free the Marines, he wasn't able to heed Evans' warning quickly enough and took a bullet to the base of his skull.

He lost consciousness on impact and crashed to the deck of their landing craft. Without time to check on his friend, Evans took the wheel and sped them through the water back to Lunga Point. If Douglas had done the same minutes earlier, he would have survived, but dozens of Marines surely wouldn't have.

Douglas was Evans' first and only concern when he beached the boat, and as he reached him, he realized that his friend had momentarily regained consciousness. Douglas' only concern was the Marines that he'd laid his life down for, asking, "Did they get off?" and only passing away once Evans had reassured him that they had with a nod (Terrell, 2016).

Douglas Munro passed away at the tender age of 22 years of age with a relieved smile on his face.

The Aftermath of the Act

With the Marines free, the extraction was complete with far fewer casualties than there could have been.

Douglas was buried on Guadalcanal the day following his heroic death, September 28, 1942. His grave was fittingly marked by a cross made by his best friend, Evans. In 1947, Douglas' remains were recovered and re-interred at Laurel Hill Memorial Park in Cle Elum a year later.

A Lasting Legacy

Douglas became the only U.S. Coast Guard to receive the military's highest honor when the Medal of Honor was presented to his proud mother in 1943. The citation for which reads:

> For extraordinary heroism and conspicuous gallantry in action above and beyond the call of duty as petty officer in charge of a group of 24 Higgins boats, engaged in the evacuation of a battalion of marines trapped by enemy Japanese forces at Point Cruz, Guadalcanal on 27 September 1942. After making preliminary plans for the evacuation of nearly 500 beleaguered marines, Munro, under constant strafing by enemy machine guns on the island, and at great risk of his life, daringly led five of his small craft toward the shore.
>
> As he closed the beach, he signaled the others to land, and then in order to draw the enemy's fire and protect the heavily loaded boats, he valiantly placed his craft with its two small guns as a shield between the beachhead and the Japanese. When the perilous task of evacuation was nearly completed, Munro was instantly

> killed by enemy fire, but his crew, two of whom were wounded, carried on until the last boat had loaded and cleared the beach. By his outstanding leadership, expert planning, and dauntless devotion to duty, he and his courageous comrades undoubtedly saved the lives of many who otherwise would have perished. He gallantly gave his life for his country. (Munro, 2024)

His Medal of Honor was supplemented by the following awards (Munro, 2024):

- Purple Heart
- Coast Guard Good Conduct Medal
- American Campaign Medal
- American Defense Service Medal
- World War II Victory Medal
- Asiatic-Pacific Campaign Medal with one Battle Star

Douglas has also been honored inside of the military. With three warships named after him, three coast guard facilities, and several monuments erected of him—one of which, at the Training Center in Cape May, is used by Coast Guard recruits as a gathering place on the anniversary of his death, during which a trio of volleys are fired in his honor.

He also holds the esteemed honor of being the only non-Marine represented on the Wall of Heroes in the National Museum of Marine Corps.

Outside of the military, he is also honored by the hometown where he used to lug wood around so selflessly, with a boulevard named after him.

Douglas' gravesite was expanded by the city of Cle Elum in 1954 with the fitting installation of two decommissioned Mk22 naval deck guns on each side of his grave, and with his parents being buried next to the son that they were so proud of.

Douglas' childhood best friend, Mike Cooley, spent more than 30 years walking three miles from his home to his fallen friend's gravesite so that he could raise and lower the United States flag. Even when Cooley had pneumonia, he braved the walk to honor his friend.

When Cooley passed away in 1999, a lighted flagpole was erected at Douglas' gravesite so that the proud colors of the United States that he fought so valiantly for could be on display all year round. Cooley's ashes were interred at the Douglas' burial site, reuniting the friends.

With the erection of the lighted flagpole also came an annual military ceremony at Douglas' grave site on the anniversary of his death.

I think there's truly something to be said of the fact that Douglas was held in such high esteem by both Mike Cooley and Ray Evans.

Douglas Munro sacrificed his young life for countless marines, and even in his dying moments, he was only concerned for the lives of others.

Chapter 24:

James Megellas

United States Army, Battle of the Bulge, 1945

It was not until our men witnessed this that we fully realized what we had been fighting for. The destruction of the monstrosity the Nazis had created was the cause greater than ourselves that we had often alluded to but never fully understood. It was a defining moment in our lives: who we were, what we believed in, and what we stood for. –James Megellas

Background of the Hero

James Megellas was born on March 11, 1917, in Wisconsin. Born into a Greek-American family, he grew up in the city of Fond du Lac and attended the local high school before attending the nearby Ripon College.

It wouldn't take long before James was thrust into the reality of the war that America was facing when Pearl Harbor was attacked halfway through his senior year. He made his intentions crystal clear when he responded by enrolling in the College's Reserve Officers' Training Corps program. James wanted to fight for his country.

He received a commission as a second lieutenant upon his graduation in May of 1942, with his first assignment being to join the Signal Corps and help design and develop the vital communication equipment needed for the American soldiers.

James didn't want to develop equipment; he wanted to fight and very quickly volunteered as a paratrooper so that he could get out of the laboratories and onto the field of combat.

The Heroic Act

In October of 1943, just 17 months after his graduation, James would get his wish and join the 504 Parachute Infantry Regiment of the 82nd Airborne Division.

He was thrust into combat that same year when he took to the skies as a member of H Company, 3rd Battalion. While facing heavy combat in the mountains of Naples, Italy, his resolve would be tested early into his service when he was struck by fragments of a German hand grenade and needed evacuation from the battlefield.

After receiving treatment, he swiftly rejoined his team for Operation Shingle, during which he traded his parachute for a landing craft and fought to take control of the Italian coastal town of Anzio.

While James and his brothers would eventually gain control of Rome from their Axis enemy, the victory would come at both a personal cost when James was shot through the arm at point-blank range and left badly wounded. And a much greater cost in the form of 30,000 Allied casualties.

The losses for James' 504 regiment were so heavy, in fact, that they didn't join the rest of the 82nd Division during the invasion of Normandy. After a little rest, James and the surviving members of the 504 were headed to the Netherlands for Operation Market Garden.

Operation Market Garden was an Allied attempt to both liberate Holland, and to create an invasion route into northern Germany. The operation did result in the Allies capturing the cities of Nijmegen and Eindhoven, and a handful of towns. However, the Allies fell short of their ultimate goal of securing the bridge over the Rhine at Arnhem.

Once James and his brothers had landed as safely as possible, they were faced with an incredibly daunting prospect. To reach their goal in the heart of the Netherlands, they were first going to have to cross the heavily covered Waal River and relieve their Allied brothers, who were pinned down on bridges on the north side of the Rhine.

The men required to cross that day, including James, knew that they were essentially fish in a barrel and that their flimsy canvas boats were barely even capable of making the journey. When they undertook the near-impossible crossing for their country, most wouldn't complete the journey. Somehow, despite their boats providing little cover and the daylight providing even less,

James was able to survive the river crossing under the constant, murderous machine gun fire of the awaiting Germans. Camped down in the Nazi-controlled Netherlands two short weeks after the daring crossing of the Waal (the Allies didn't have enough boats for all of their men to retreat in one go), he was able to bravely immobilize a German observation post and machine gun nest all on his own.

While Operation Market Garden was ultimately a misstep, James' next assignment would not be. In late December 1944, he headed to Belgium to engage in the Battle of the Bulge, and the end was near for Germany.

First, James rescued one of his wounded brothers at the base of a hill near Cheneux after defeating an enemy despite their having the advantageous high ground. Then, while enduring ice-cold temperatures and exhaustingly deep snow, James and his platoon pressed toward the Belgian town of Herresbach on January 28, 1945.

The Americans appeared to initially have had some good fortune, springing a surprise on 200 Germans on their way out of the town. With the element of surprise on their side, the Americans were able to inflict devastating damage on their foes.

The Germans who were unable to flee were either killed or captured, and the path appeared to have been cleared for an assault on the town. What the Americans hadn't realized, however, was that a German Mark V Panther tank was taking aim, and they were in grave danger.

James sprang into action, sprinting directly toward the tank and disabling it with the toss of a single grenade. With the tank disabled at his hand, James then triumphantly climbed atop the beast and sunk a second grenade deep into its heart, shattering all inside, as well as the German resistance inside of the town of Herresbach.

When the dust had settled that day, the town had been seized without a single casualty inflicted on James' platoon—an outcome which would have been impossible if that tank had managed to open fire.

The Aftermath of the Act

The Battle of the Bulge paved the way for James and his platoon to advance on to Germany, where they liberated the Wöbbelin concentration camp and were confronted face-to-face with the true horrors of the Holocaust, including bodies stacked up waiting for burial and survivors that weighed less than 65 pounds (Caltrider, 2022).

Following James' actions, he led his rifle company, Company H, 504 PIR, down New York's Fifth Avenue in a Victory Parade.

After rightfully basking in the glory, James left the active Army that same year, having achieved the rank of captain. He served in the Army Reserve for another 16 years and, from 1946 to 1978, served with the United States Agency for International Development (USAID), including two tours in the Vietnam War. He had reached the rank of lieutenant colonel by the time of his full retirement.

The desire to serve the American public continued to burn deeply in James, and he served on the Fond du Lac city council until 1961, during which time he also made a couple of unsuccessful attempts to represent the 6th District of Wisconsin as a Democrat in 1958 and 1960. It was in May of 1962 that James would marry Carole Margaret Laehn, the true love of his life. The pair had two children and four grandchildren. James reached his 100th birthday in 2017 and died three years later—22 days after he had turned 103. Carole died that same year at the age of 83.

A Lasting Legacy

James died as the most decorated officer in the history of the 82nd Airborne (*Colonel James Megellas*, n.d.).

His most prestigious accolade must be considered the Silver Star (with one oak leaf cluster) which he was awarded on the 19th of March 1945. The citation for which is included below:

> The President of the United States of America, authorized by Act of Congress July 9, 1918, takes pleasure in presenting the Silver Star to First Lieutenant (Infantry) James Megellas (ASN:0-439607), United States Army, for gallantry in action while serving with Company H, 3d Battalion, 504th Parachute Infantry Regiment, 82d Airborne Division, in action on 28 January 1945, near Herresbach, Belgium. After breaking a trail across country for twelve hours in deep, dry snow, First Lieutenant Megellas, a platoon leader, was ordered to advance with his platoon and two supporting tanks along the main road leading into Herrebach.
>
> About one mile from the town, his platoon was fired upon by about 200 Germans forming a defense. Quickly grasping the situation, he led a frontal attack on the startled enemy who attempted to fight back. First Lieutenant Megellas' direction and leadership of his men was so superb that within ten minutes the entire force of enemy was either killed, captured, or fled into the town. He then reorganized his platoon, and with the two supporting tanks followed the enemy into the town. Braving heavy enemy sniper and rifle fire, he personally took a leading part in flushing the enemy out of their houses, killing eight and capturing five enemy. As a result of First Lieutenant Megellas' fierce leadership and skillful handing of his men, over 100

> enemy were killed, 180 captured, and large amounts of valuable equipment fell into our hands. This feat was accomplished without the loss of a single man wounded or killed. First Lieutenant Megellas demonstrated a remarkable degree of tactical skill and a brand of courageous leadership which reflects highly upon himself and the Airborne Forces. (Megellas, 2024)

As of the time of writing, James' Silver Star has not been upgraded to a Medal of Honor despite several bills suggesting that it should. Hopefully this is something that will now happen posthumously.

He had a huge collection of other awards and accolades bestowed upon of which he can be justly proud, including (Megellas, 2024):

- Combat Infantryman Badge
- Distinguished Service Cross
- Bronze Star Medal (with one oak cluster and a "V" representing valor and heroism)
- Purple Heart (with one oak leaf cluster)
- American Defense Service Medal
- Presidential Unit Citation (with one oak leaf cluster)
- American Campaign Medal
- European-African-Middle Eastern Campaign Medal (with one silver and bronze star)
- Army of Occupation Medal

- National Defense Service Medal
- World War II Victory Medal
- Armed Forces Reserve Medal
- Belgian Fourragere
- Vietnam Service Medal (with two bronze stars)
- Republic of Vietnam Campaign Medal
- DAR Medal of Honor
- Dallas Military Ball's Meritorious Service Award
- Order of Saint Maurice

James was also given the honor of being the first American to be awarded the Military Order of William Orange Lanyard by the Netherlands' Government. Handpicked as the most outstanding officer of his Division, the award was presented in 1945 by Major Dr. Jan de Quay, the Dutch Minister of War.

He was also portrayed on the big screen in the 1977 movie *A Bridge Too Far,* which depicts his daring attempt to cross the Rhine.

James took steps to ensure that he would shape the legacy he was leaving behind when he penned a memoir in 2003 titled *All the Way to Berlin: A Paratrooper at War in Europe.*

James Megellas' swift disablement of a tank ensured the lives of his entire platoon, but perhaps more impressive was the tactical skill and composure that he showed in leading his platoon to successful missions without losing a single life.

Chapter 25:

Lee Miller

Photographer and War Correspondent, Europe, 1942–1945

Nearly all the photographs I ever took have disappeared—lost in New York!—thrown away by the Germans—in Paris—bombed and burned in the London blitz—and now I find Condé Nast has just casually scrapped everything I did for them, including war pictures. –Lee Miller

Content Warning: This chapter includes themes of sexual assault that may be disturbing to some. Please read on with caution.

Background of the Hero

Lee Miller was born on April 23, 1907. She was raised in Poughkeepsie, New York, by her German father, Theodore, and her mother, Florence, who was of Irish and Scottish descent. She was the middle child, with a younger brother, Erik, and an older brother named Johnny.

Lee faced horrors from a tender age and was raped when she was seven years old. The assault was exacted by a friend of her parents and saw her infected with gonorrhea. Unsurprisingly, this had lasting effects, and Lee would struggle mentally throughout the rest of her childhood.

Following her traumatic experience, she was expelled from every school that she attended throughout her childhood in Poughkeepsie and struggled for direction and stability. One constant source of stability that she did benefit from, however, was her close relationship with her father. It was her father who would first introduce her to photography, as he himself worked as an amateur stereoscopic photographer.

Lee posed for her father from a young age, which was perhaps what sparked her interest in the arts and inspired her to move to Paris in 1925 when she was 18. Once there, she studied at the Ladislas Medgyes School of Stagecraft.

Lee had found her calling, and when she returned home the following year, she soon enrolled in an experimental drama program at Vassar College. She had become infatuated with the arts and would leave home again that same year so that she could study painting and life drawing at Manhattan's *Arts*

Students League of New York. When Lee was 19 years old, she met the publisher of *Vogue* in an incredible twist of fate when he prevented her from stepping out in front of a moving car. This meeting would be the first big break that she received in her career, and a modeling career would soon follow.

Lee was a sensation in the fashion world and found herself on the cover of *Vogue* in her first year working as a model. She spent two years as one of the most sought-after models in New York, during which time she worked with a who's who of leading fashion photographers. She kept her feet on the ground, though, and saw this as an opportunity to make key contacts in her career. She was much more interested in working on the other side of the camera and aspired to a career like those shooting her.

With the goal of becoming a renowned photographer, Lee studied under Man Ray, a now legendary American visual artist who contributed significantly to both the Dada and Surrealist movements.

Her journey to become Man Ray's student wasn't an easy one and only came to fruition because of her determination. Having traveled back to Paris in 1929, Lee was initially turned away and told he didn't take on students.

She knew where she wanted to be and simply refused to take no for an answer. Eventually, Man Ray gave in, and the two fell into a passionate love affair fueled by their artistic pursuits. Lee soon opened her own photographic studio and helped Man Ray with fashion assignments to free him up to focus on his paintings.

The pair's work became intertwined at that time, and it was during that period that Lee accidentally discovered the photographic technique of *solarization* when she switched a light on during the development of her film.

Solarization became a signature technique of the couple's work, and Lee had undoubtedly carved a significant career for herself within the photography world. She was running in circles so influential that they included Pablo Picasso and Salvador Dali.

It won't surprise many reading this that Lee's rise wasn't without experiencing misogyny, and she had to constantly fight to ensure her work was taken seriously.

When her relationship with Man Ray turned sour, she returned home to New York and opened a new photography studio with her younger brother, Erik. Her career continued to flourish, and she worked with powerful clients and regularly featured as part of prestigious exhibitions.

It wasn't until 1934, when Lee married an Egyptian businessman, that her life would take its next sharp detour. While living in Cairo, her work as a photographer took a backseat; however, she did take pictures of the vast Egyptian desert.

While her time in Egypt offered her a reprieve from her busy life and career, she found herself longing for a return to Paris and missing the frantic nature of her career. She was bored, and perhaps she took the peace she'd found for granted because the next move she would make would shape her destiny and forever change her life.

The Heroic Act

Unlike most of the heroes within this book, it wouldn't be the attack on Pearl Harbor that dragged Lee into the Second World War. When London was bombed in 1940, she was living in Hampstead with a new partner who she had met upon her return to Paris. Despite the pleas from her family and friends to return home to the United States, she had other ideas and wanted to use her photography skills to ensure the horrors facing Londoners were documented. With England's capital desperately scrambling to weather the storm of the Blitz, Lee met with the editor of *Vogue* and offered her services as a photographer. She was turned down initially; however, the magazine believed that Lee could be a beneficial contributor as a studio assistant.

This was quite humbling for Lee, of course, who had reached dizzying heights in her career to this point and ran multiple successful studios. However, she checked her ego at the door and decided to maximize the opportunity to get her foot in it.

When many of *Vogue's* male photographers left to fight on the front lines, an opportunity presented itself for Lee to work in the magazine's fashion and lifestyle division. Work in that division may sound inconsequential now, but at the time, the British government saw these magazines as a crucial resource in helping their women cope with the devastating effects of the war.

In 1941, Britain was struggling and deemed the conscription of women necessary. This gave women the choice between working in industrial settings or providing nursing services. It was all hands on deck for the population of London, and Lee was leading the charge to ensure that the sacrifice of women across the country was documented and celebrated.

Under her hand, *Vogue* morphed from a luxurious fashion magazine to an outlet for serious news and one that celebrated the efforts of women on the front lines. She wrote several pieces that showcased women contributing to Britain's war effort, including features on nurses at an army base in Oxford and the all-female British Army artillery unit—the Auxiliary Territorial Service. Lee's work not only inspired the public but also built a feeling of unity and camaraderie in a country that desperately needed it.

As the war grew in intensity, and America found itself dragged into the violence, Lee was made an accredited photographer for the U.S. Army and started to work as a war correspondent, a role that saw her move from the photography studio to the front lines.

She took up her new role without hesitation and was paired with established American war photographer, David Scherman. Scherman had been working for the American magazine *Life* and fulfilled a similar role that Lee had with *Vogue*. Scherman was tasked with taking Lee under his wing, and she was more than willing to grab the opportunity.

She was thrust onto the frontlines as one of only a handful of female army photographers to see battle. She was equipped with a steel helmet that was specifically designed to enable her to use her camera comfortably and effectively.

Lee traveled to France less than a month after D-Day, and after documenting the chaotic aftermath of the Allied victory, was later tasked with reporting on the American Army nurses working in a field hospital close to Omaha Beach.

She documented the heroic liberations of Alsace and later, France as a whole, including poignantly capturing the shaming of French women who were accused of siding with the Germans, and had their heads shaved and foreheads marked with Swastikas.

A breakdown in military communication resulted in Lee being trapped in St. Malo and facing heavy besiegement. She watched and documented the strength of American troops assaulting the German-held port.

At that time, women war correspondents weren't allowed to join the front lines, and while the breakdown in communication wasn't her doing, she found herself being placed under temporary arrest before being completely barred from the front lines. Lee spent the following months in France and Luxembourg, continuing to capture images of the effects of the carnage inflicted on the countries and their people. She felt that she still had a duty to tell the whole story of the war, though, and when she got word that the concentration camp in Buchenwald had been liberated, she hitched a ride there and reconnected with the U.S. Army.

Even once she was faced with the unimaginable horrors of the Nazi concentration camps of Buchenwald and later Dachau, she refused to be deterred and became even more defiant in her mission to spread the reality of the crimes that the Axis were exacting at that time. Conceding that while she didn't typically capture horrors with her photography, she felt strongly that the Axis' atrocities were so rife that they had to be seen (Villa, 2021).

When Lee sent photos of the horrors she had seen in the Nazi concentration camps back to *Vogue,* she pleaded for the photographs to be published and implored her editors to believe what their eyes were showing them.

Vogue published Lee's photographs to their previously disbelieving British and American audiences, who had perhaps dismissed written accounts as propaganda. The photos couldn't be dismissed, nor could the defiantly written headline "Believe it" that accompanied them (Villa, 2021).

Ironically, given Lee's past as a model and her desire to be behind the camera instead of in front of it, it was a photo of her in Hitler's bathtub that is perhaps now seen as her most iconic. Following the liberation of the Dachau concentration camp, both Lee and Scherman visited Hitler's apartment in the city of Munich. After muddying his bathroom floor with the dirt of Dachau, Lee took a bath in Hitler's tub and slept in his bed. Incredibly, Lee's visit to Hitler's apartment took place on the day of his suicide.

Despite the defiance of her visit to Hitler's apartment, her job wasn't yet finished. She continued to capture the harrowing aftermath of Germany's actions. Her work at this time included photos of a Nazi deputy and his family committing suicide, dying children in a Vienna hospital, the reality of peasant life in Hungary following the war, and thousands of Nazi corpses strewn alongside their families.

Aftermath of the Act

Given the atrocities she was faced with, it's no surprise that Lee spoke very rarely of her experiences following the war. After continuing to work for *Vogue* for a further two years, she quietly moved back to Britain.

She was struggling with her mental health and suffered from clinical depression and post-traumatic stress disorder. As she spiraled, she turned to heavy drinking to numb her mental anguish.

She married for the second time on May 3, 1947, and her only son was born in September 1947. She found solace in the arts that had captured her attention before the war and bought a farm in the county of Sussex with her husband. The farm was visited by artistic icons from her past, such as Pablo Picasso, Man Ray, and Max Ernst.

Lee eventually left photography in the past as she struggled to separate the artistry from the horrors that she captured in the concentration camps. She refused the suggestions of those around her to promote her work and was desperate to leave it in the past.

Without the knowledge of mental health that we are privileged with today, Lee was without the help she desperately needed as she plunged into a downward spiral.

Lee died of cancer in 1977, aged 70, at her Farley farmhouse, where she'd isolated herself during the end of her life. After her cremation, her ashes were spread on the grounds of her farm.

A Lasting Legacy

Despite her humility, Lee's artistic work has inspired Gucci's Ann Demeulemeester, Alexander McQueen, and Frida Giannini. Academy Award-winning screenwriter and celebrated playwright, David Hare, praised Lee's willingness to shock people out of their comfort zone to spread her message (Giovanni, 2007).

While Lee rarely promoted her own work, her proud son Anthony has worked diligently since the early 1980s to understand, conserve, and promote her legacy. His research into his mother's work led to the discovery of more than 60,000 pieces of work. These pieces included negatives, journals, souvenirs, photographs, and love letters that had all been boxed up and locked away safely in the attic of their farm.

In 1985, he published a biography of his mother's work titled *The Lives of Lee Miller,* which was followed by a number of books written by different art historians and writers. In 1992, he also collaborated with David Scherman, his mother's former partner, on *Lee Miller's War: Photographer and Correspondent with the Allies in Europe 1944-45.*

Anthony was also interviewed for the creation of a documentary about his mother in 1995, and he was consulted on an audiobook about his mother's influence on surrealism, too. Today, he proudly offers tours of the Sussex farm that include displays of her private works.

Lee's son's dedication to his mother's legacy has ensured that she wasn't forgotten.

A blue plaque has been attached to Lee's Hampstead residence in her honor. In 2005, a biography was published about her life, and her life story was also turned into a musical in the same year.

Two years later, an interactive CD and DVD were created that explored her life and photography, and in 2015, an exhibition of her work was erected in the Scottish National Portrait Gallery.

A work of historical fiction was also published in 2019 based on Lee's life and her relationship with Man Ray. And finally, in 2023, Kate Winslet starred as Lee in the movie *Lee,* directed by Ellen Kuras, and based on the 1985 biography written by her son, Anthony Penrose.

Lee Miller's work will always live on, serving as a reminder of both the importance of world peace and the horrors of war.

Chapter 26:

Norman Kleiss

United States Navy, Battle of Midway, 1942

I must say, the sight of the Hiryu*'s destruction seared itself into my memory. Even now I can close my eyes and see the image of the mutilated flight deck clear as day. It's probably my most vivid recollection of the battle.* –Norman Kleiss

Background of the Hero

Norman Kleiss was born on March 7, 1916, to parents John and Lulu Kleiss. He grew up in the small town of Coffeyville in Kansas, a stone's throw from the Oklahoma border.

For Norman, there was little else that mattered more than serving his country. At the age of just 15, he joined the Kansas National Guard in 1931, serving in the 114th Cavalry Regiment before enrolling at the United States Naval Academy when he was 18.

Norman was laser-focused. Four years later, he graduated from the Academy among a class of 438 midshipmen. Little did he know that he would soon be one of 421 in that class who would be called upon to fight in World War II.

At the time, the Navy required all graduates to serve in the surface fleet for a minimum of two years before they could attend flight training. Norman's service as part of that fleet saw him set sail on three ships between June 1938 and April 1940: the *USS Goff, USS Yarnall,* and the *USS Vincennes.*

Norman served with the same competence and respect that proved him to be a reliable graduate. He was so reliable, in fact, that as soon as he completed his two-year service period, he was undergoing psychological and physical tests and heading to Naval Air Station Pensacola for flight training.

Norman passed his training with flying colors, if you'll excuse the pun, and didn't suffer a single crash. He was a natural, and after 11 months of training, earned his wings on April 27, 1941, just a month after his 25th birthday. Norman had spent the decade since the tender age of 15 serving his country, and now, he was ready to fly. He was assigned to the *USS Enterprise's* Scouting Squadron Six (VS-6), a scout-bombing squadron.

The reality of Norman's assignment sunk in when the *USS Enterprise* set sail for Pearl Harbor in early May, and Norman and the rest of his squadron started training for war. While getting familiar with the two-seater scout bomber assigned to him, Norman was tasked with practicing dive bombing, navigation, and gunnery. He excelled throughout training and was promoted to the rank of a junior grade lieutenant just a month later.

With Europe already locked in battle and World War II having raged for two bloody years already, it would be misguided to suggest that Norman wasn't expecting to fight for his country in the near future. However, I'd wager that he wasn't expecting to be thrust into the middle of a war just eight months after earning his wings.

The Heroic Act

Norman and the rest of Scouting Six had initially scrambled to engage with Japanese fighters during Pearl Harbor. However, while his squadron did lose six pilots and gunners, our hero didn't encounter any Japanese planes. He was caught in a spot of friendly fire when he was mistaken for a Japanese dive bomber, though! Thankfully, Norman was able to negotiate that sticky situation to fly and fight another day.

It wasn't until February 1 that Norman himself engaged in his first battle of World War II and marked the first bookmark in what would culminate as a truly remarkable run of bombings from a single pilot.

Norman took flight from the *USS Enterprise* on February 1st and formed part of an air strike that was targeting a Japanese base at Kwajalein Atoll. It was during the air strike that he would drop his first meaningful bombs on the Japanese, first immobilizing a parked plane at Roi Airfield with the force of his wing bombs and then claiming his first major target by obliterating the light Japanese cruiser *Katori* with a 500-pound undercarriage bomb.

Norman was suddenly in the thick of a highly destructive and successful run.

After refueling and rearming at the *Enterprise,* Norman then joined another fleet of SBD planes; this time, their target was the Japanese base on Taroa Island. Taroa Island was the home to a major Japanese Airfield, Taroa Airfield, and represented an opportunity to put a sizable dent in the Japanese fleet.

Their raid was successful and lit the fuse for what was going to be the slow-burning process of starving the Japanese base of resources. It was going to take time, though, and Norman's squadron didn't successfully attack such a fortified base without casualty.

Norman's SBD was struck by heavy machine-gun fire, and his gunner was wounded, too.

Just a month later, Norman would take flight in another major way when he formed part of the team that raided Wake Island on the 24th of February. He helped bomb key structures on the island and then, barely two weeks later, did the same to Marcus Island.

Norman and the other U.S. dive bombers weren't just chipping away at the Japanese fortress; they were taking huge chunks from them, serving as a first wave of attack that cleared the way for ground troops to advance.

If Norman's story ended here, he would already be considered a hero. However, his most heroic act was remarkably still to come.

Between June 4–7, Norman took flight for the Battle of Midway, and once the dust had settled and engines had cooled, he helped swing things in his country's favor.

In 1942, the Japanese domination of the Pacific Ocean was a real problem for the Allies and was underpinned by a major fleet of aircraft carriers that the Japanese had long had at their disposal.

The Battle of Midway was a major naval battle that presented the United States with an opportunity to cut into that fleet, and they were sure to take their chance.

For Norman, the orders were much easier to deliver than they would be to execute—destroy the Japanese carrier fleet and cripple them in the process.

On the sunny morning of June 4th, Norman took flight alongside 32 other SBD dive bombers and began searching for the Japanese carrier task force. After hours of searching, and with the bombers on the brink of giving up on their search due to a combination of low plane fuel and pilot fatigue, they caught a glimpse of precisely what they had been searching for—the Japanese destroyer, *Arashi.*

After pursuing the *Arashi* for merely minutes, their persistence was repaid when they were led right to the main body of the Japanese fleet, including the *Kaga*—an imposing Japanese aircraft carrier and their number one target.

Better yet, the *Kaga* was lined with planes refueling and reloading, meaning the Japanese were vulnerable and could offer little resistance to the Americans' aerial assault.

It was at 10:22 a.m. when Scouting Six commenced their attack on the vulnerable *Kaga,* and Norman would have a meaningful role to play in the devastating bombing run. He was the second pilot to score a significant hit, making his descent from 20,000 feet and destroying several Japanese aircraft with perfectly placed wing-tip bombs at the front of the *Kaga's* flight deck. Norman struck again, dropping his 500-pound bomb payload through the decks of the carrier, which crashed through the Rising Sun insignia on deck and descended through the decks like a knife through the layers of a tiramisu.

Crucially, Norman's bomb also connected with the torpedoes below the decks of the powerful carrier and detonated them simultaneously, erupting the craft into a ball of flames. The *Kaga* was down, but Norman nearly went with it when he narrowly avoided crashing into the ocean in the aftermath of his bullseye!

In just five minutes, three United States dive bomber squadrons had dealt fatal damage to three of the four Japanese aircraft carriers. Had they not found the Japanese armada at this point, the entire outcome of the Battle of Midway could have been very different.

After returning to the *Enterprise* for a nap and lunch, refueling and rearming his plane, Norman took to the skies once more. This time, Scouting Six had a new target: the mammoth aircraft carrier *Hiryu,* and things were going to be a little trickier.

More nimble than other Japanese carriers, *Hiryu* took evasive action, forcing Norman to use all of his nous and skill to track it down before dropping his payload as one of the carriers turned to ensure he struck it with aplomb—*bullseye!*

Norman later explained the way that the destructive images from that day are seared into his memory: "[E]ven now I can close my eyes and see the image of the mutilated flight deck clear as day. It's probably my most vivid recollection of the battle" (*The Words of War*, para 4, 2018). He would accompany another fleet on his third run of the Battle of Midway the next day on June 5.

While this run was unsuccessful and they failed to register a hit on a destroyer, the *Tanikaze*, Norman's fleet was undeterred and sunk the cruiser, *Mikuma,* the very next day. Norman scored with another direct hit near the smokestack of the craft, making him the only pilot to score three direct hits during the battle, cementing his legacy as a key warrior in a key victory.

By the end of the Battle of Midway, Japan had lost four carriers and thousands of their men, including some of their best pilots. Comparatively, the United States had lost just one carrier and 360 men (*Battle of Midway,* 2019).

The Aftermath of the Act

When Norman returned to the *Enterprise* and docked back at Pearl Harbor, he would learn that his role in the war as a combatant was over. Throughout World War II, the United States had been rotating their experienced pilots in and out of the battlefield so that they could train rookies, giving the rookies the best training and the experienced pilots a rest.

This innovative policy would be key for the Allies moving forward, as once the more experienced pilots of the Axis fell, they were left with only untrained rookies to replace them.

Norman married his beloved Eunice Marie "Jean" Machon in Las Vegas in 1942, less than a month after the Battle of Midway, in which he'd been such a significant player. At that point, he transitioned to a career on shore. He served as Assistant Head of Structures Branch at the Bureau of Aeronautics before eventually being promoted to Head of the Structures Branch. He then made his next meaningful career change in 1949, when he became the Bureau of Aeronautics representative at the Lockheed Corporation in Burbank, California—a role that saw him supervise Navy aircraft engineers, aircraft inspectors, and test pilots.

Norman eventually retired from his fruitful Navy career in 1962 as a captain, at which point he transitioned to working as a senior staff engineer at Allegany Ballistics Laboratory. He then worked as a part-time surveyor before wrapping up his employment as a teacher at Berkeley Springs High School.

Norman and his wife moved into the retirement community of Air Force Village in 1997, where they lived together until her death in 2006, ending a beautiful marriage that lasted 64 years. Norman would live another 10 years before passing away less than two months after celebrating his 100th birthday.

He was buried beside his wife at Fort Sam Houston National Cemetery and was survived by two sons, two daughters, seven grandchildren, and ten great-grandchildren.

A Lasting Legacy

When Norman turned 99, he made the decision to cement his own legacy—not as a dive bomber, but as a writer. He decided to pen a memoir titled *Never Call Me a Hero: A Legendary Dive-Bomber Pilot Remembers the Battle of Midway*, to ensure that his fallen comrades got their just due. It's within that memoir that Kleiss very humbly claims that he's simply a "lucky fool" (*The Words of War*, para 9, 2018).

Norman Kleiss received a prestigious Navy Cross for his incredible career, the citation for which reads:

> The President of the United States of America takes pleasure in presenting the Navy Cross to Lieutenant, Junior Grade Norman Jack Kleiss, United States Navy, for extraordinary heroism in operations against the enemy while serving as Pilot of a carrier-based Navy Scouting Plane of Scouting Squadron SIX (VS-6), attached to the U.S.S. ENTERPRISE (CV-6), during

> the "Air Battle of Midway," against enemy Japanese forces on 4 - 6 June 1942. Participating in a devastating assault against a Japanese invasion fleet, Lieutenant, Junior Grade, Kleiss, with fortitude and resolute devotion to duty, pressed home his attacks in the face of a formidable barrage of anti-aircraft fire and fierce fighter opposition. His gallant perseverance and utter disregard for his own personal safety were important contributing factors to the success achieved by our forces and were in keeping with the highest traditions of the United States Naval Service. (Kleiss, 2024)

His Navy Cross was supplemented by the following awards (Kleiss, 2024):

- Naval Aviator Badge
- Distinguished Flying Cross
- Air Medal
- Navy Presidential Unit Citation with one Bronze Star
- American Defense Service Medal with one Bronze Star
- American Campaign Medal
- World War II Victory Medal
- National Defense Service Medal
- Asiatic-Pacific Campaign Medal with four Bronze Stars

The victory the United States claimed in the Battle of Midway prevented Japan from growing throughout the Pacific Ocean and ensured that their own troops could cut down travel time to the ever-shrinking Japanese empire.

Norman Kleiss played a vital role in the United States' ability to achieve that victory, and he should be forever celebrated for the precision and courage he showed.

Chapter 27:

George Watson

United States Army, Porlock Harbor, New Guinea, 1943

I think it might be an appropriate way to close to say that when I gave Mr. Watson's medal to the Sergeant Major of the Army, he looked at it and smiled and he said, 'This is indicative of the type of soldiers we have today, a group of people in our military, men and women, that really do reflect the vast and rich texture of our Nation. –President Bill Clinton

Background of the Hero

George Watson was born on March 14, 1914. He was raised in Laurel, Mississippi by parents who were both sharecroppers. Naturally, George spent a lot of time outside on the farm and quickly took to swimming and fishing.

Where George's talent truly shone, though, was in mathematics. He excelled at school in the subject and wanted to go to college. However, a combination of the limited opportunities that Laurel offered and his family being hit hard by the Great Depression meant that if George was going to gain admission into college, he was going to have to do it the hard way.

Doing things the hard way wasn't something that fazed George, however, and in 1932, he made the brave decision to leave home at 17 and move to Alabama to live with his grandmother. While he may have felt that Alabama would provide him with more opportunities to progress, his main reason for leaving was to leave his own parents with one less mouth to feed.

Alabama was also in the grips of the Great Depression, and things weren't getting any easier for George. Still, he retained his dream of going to college to study engineering. To achieve that dream, he was going to have to pay for his tuition himself, and his first step toward doing that was obtaining employment as a janitor at a private club.

The job was low-paid, but it crucially allowed him to start saving some money. He did so for two years before he started to crave more money so he could sock more away. In a bittersweet twist of fate, tragedy would strike Birmingham, Alabama, in 1934, which paved the way for George to do just that. When a large department store erupted in flames and caused more than $3 million in damages, the fire department sought to overhaul its team and hire more firefighters. George took the opportunity and was excited at the chance to provide a meaningful service to his community. In 1934, he applied to the fire service and was promptly hired. He continued saving his money diligently, never losing sight of his goal of going to college. After five years fighting fires and seven years of careful money saving, George had finally earned enough to pay his way into college and achieve his dream.

He enrolled at Engineering School at Colorado A&M in September of 1939 and was excelling. But in 1942, everything changed for George and the rest of the country. His dreams would have to be put on hold.

The Heroic Act

When George was drafted into the U.S. Army on September 1st, 1942, he was 28 years old and left his wife and daughter behind to do so. Like many, he needed no reminder of what was at stake and was fighting for the lives of his loved ones.

He underwent his basic training at Camp Lee in Virginia, where he was assigned to the second battalion of the 29th Quartermaster (QM) Regiment. The QM was focused on using analytical skills to make technical decisions and plan military supply-point operations. George's love of math and engineering background made him a perfect fit for the QM and a great asset.

George and his unit traveled to South Carolina to conclude their training before deployment on December 27, 1942. They were soon headed for Australia, and while aboard the *USS Hermitage,* George served as a bath and laundry specialist.

They traveled across the Pacific Ocean, cutting through the Panama Canal. All the while, George performed his tasks diligently and continued to prove himself a crucial member of the team.

The *Hermitage* reached Brisbane on January 31, 1943. George and the members of his regiment were soon to be put to work as members of Operation Lilliput, a key seaborne convoy operation that had commenced the month prior. The operation allowed supplies, weapons, and troops to be transported to Oro Bay in New Guinea with enough regularity that the Army would be well enough equipped to capture the Japanese beachhead at Buna-Gona.

The operation was a daring one, and you won't be surprised to read that those involved in fulfilling the operation were under constant fire from Japanese aircraft seeking to slow the Army's ability to grow in the area.

It was on March 8 that George was a passenger on the U.S Army Transport (USAT) *Jacob* when the Japanese struck with devastating effect.

The Japanese had long been targeting U.S. ships within the local shipping lanes; however, up until that point, the U.S. escort ships had managed to keep them at bay. Indeed, the escort ships had seemingly managed to do the same at 1 p.m. on March 8, too, but when the Japanese launched their second wave of attack, they penetrated the *Jacob's* defenses, leaving George and his fellow passengers in grave danger.

George, who had been out on deck breathing in the fresh sea air at the time of the alarms screaming out, must have been looking forward to returning to the solid ground of the fast-approaching Porlock Bay.

When a trio of Japanese bombs crashed through the ship's deck, sailors and soldiers alike were thrown overboard by the sickening blasts. Those who were still on board were faced with a blazing inferno that was threatening to engulf the entire ship. The first thought of those aboard was to fight the fire, but when the water pumps malfunctioned, fighting the fire and saving the *Jacob* and the crucial cargo was made impossible. When the captain ordered that all aboard should abandon the ship, George was right in the heart of the chaos. As sailors and soldiers flung themselves overboard and into the water, George had a life jacket thrust into his chest by one of his friends. He refused the jacket, knowing that he was a strong swimmer and that the jacket would be best served wrapped around the body of another.

With the ship tipping heavily to the side and rapidly being swallowed by the ocean below, George and his friend leaped off the side of it and plunged 40 feet to crash into the water below. Even in the life jacket, George's friend was forced down deep into the water by the impact of their drop, so George swam as hard as he could to rescue his friend before throwing him over the side of a nearby life raft.

George didn't even consider joining his friend on the life raft, knowing that other soldiers needed his help. One by one, he forced his heavy limbs through the water and dragged man after man to the sanctity of one of the nearby rafts.

With every life that George was able to save, he was exhausting his own energy reserves. Still, he turned his attention to the sinking *Jacob* and the swirling suction vortex its weight had created. More men were in danger of being sucked to the very depths of the ocean, and they needed his help.

George left the life rafts over his shoulder and swam as fast as his tired body would allow him toward what was left of the sinking ship, knowing that it could submerge at any moment and that when it did, it was going to suck all that were in its vicinity down with it. He saved many more floundering men who were struggling to evade the troubled waters around the wreckage, and despite being encouraged to climb aboard a life raft multiple times, he continued to rescue the lives of those around him until the *Jacob* finally sank.

Aftermath of the Act

Sadly, George had exerted so much energy saving others that when the ship went, he was at the mercy of the water's pull and simply had no strength left in his muscles to escape. He had truly given everything he had that afternoon, and his body was cruelly never recovered.

A Lasting Legacy

George's selfless actions saw him posthumously awarded the Distinguished Service Cross on June 13, 1943, making him the first African American to receive the award in World War II.

When Major General Harry F. Hazlett presented the award to George's grandmother in Alabama, he told her that her grandson had perished in the "shining splendor of high courage" and had been utterly unselfish. He also claimed George was an inspiration to the entire country (tara, 2022).

After the investigation into the racial disparity of the Army in 1997, like many other heroes in this publication, George saw his Distinguished Service Cross upgraded to a Medal of Honor. His citation reads:

> For extraordinary heroism in action on 8 March 1943. Private Watson was on board a ship which was attacked and hit by enemy bombers. When the ship was abandoned, Private Watson, instead of seeking to save himself, remained in the water assisting several soldiers who could not swim to reach the safety of the raft. This heroic action, which subsequently cost him his life, resulted in the saving of several of his comrades. Weakened by his exertions, he was dragged down by the suction of the sinking ship and was drowned.

> Private Watson’s extraordinarily valorous actions, daring leadership, and self-sacrificing devotion to his fellow-man exemplify the finest traditions of military service. (Private George Watson’s Medal of Honor, 2022)

George's Medal of Honor is displayed in Virginia's U.S. Army Quartermaster Museum and was supplemented by the following awards (Watson, 2024):

- Purple Heart
- Army Good Conduct Medal
- American Campaign Medal
- European-African-Middle Eastern Campaign Medal with one 3/16" Bronze Star
- World War II Victory Medal

George has also been honored at the Walls of the Missing in the Manila American Cemetery in the Philippines, as well as having multiple places and structures named after him, including a field in Fort Moore, and two U.S. Navy ships.

George Watson sacrificed his own life to drag his brothers onto lifeboats and refused to quit until he'd rescued as many as his tired body would allow. He should be remembered as a truly selfless human being who showed the highest form of courage.

Chapter 28:

José López

United States Army, Battle of the Bulge, 1944

Everyone was afraid of where I put them to fight the Germans, I told them that they had to stop and fight back. –José López

Background of the Hero

José López was born in Mexico in 1910 and was raised by his mother, who made her living as a seamstress. José grew up very close to his mother, which certainly made her death from tuberculosis when he was just eight years old both devastating and debilitating for his young life.

Having never met his father, José effectively became an orphan when his mother died, and having initially lived with a teenage uncle in Mexico, he decided to hitchhike to Texas at just 13 years old so that he could live with a different one.

As an immigrant living in the United States, José had to adapt and become tough quickly, faced with the typical hazing and bullying that children in such situations often experience.

It was perhaps the aforementioned bullying that saw José leave school at a young age and never return. Instead, he picked up several low-income jobs, from picking cotton in the Rio Grande Valley to hopping on freight trains so that he could find odd jobs all over the country.

For José, traveling was a necessity from a young age, and it was something he became comfortable with very quickly.

He eventually took up boxing. Once he had committed to the sport, he found that he had a real talent for it. Having found his calling, he soon caught the attention of a boxing promoter when he was 17 while scrapping in a street brawl in Atlanta.

José's career took off with a bang, and he was soon traveling the world and fighting as a lightweight. He fought in 55 boxing bouts across a seven-year period under the moniker of *Kid Mendoza* and won 52 times, losing just three (Oliver, 2005). He was going to need all of the toughness and fight that he'd absorbed from his boxing career later, but before he enlisted in the United States Army, he was encouraged to join the Merchant Marines by a group of them that had watched him fight in a bout in Australia. Having purchased a fake birth certificate that stated he was born in Texas, José signed a contract to join the Merchant Marines. He was officially accepted into their union in 1936 and then spent the next five years sailing the world as a Merchant Marine. It was on a merchant ship, in fact, that José first learned of the attack on Pearl Harbor.

Despite not being present, José would be personally impacted by the attack when the merchant ship that he was sailing on arrived in California, and he was accused of being Japanese. After some convincing, he was free to go, and it's a good thing that the authorities didn't arrest José that day because he was going to be a key player in defeating the enemy that they were trying to prevent from entering their country.

José's participation in the fight was never in doubt. He immediately applied for a draft card and returned home to Brownsville in Texas, where he married his girlfriend Emilia in 1942. He received his draft card that same year and enlisted in the Army in San Antonio. José's basic training took place across Fort Sam Houston in Texas and Camp Roberts in California. After the completion of it, he was then assigned to M Company, 23rd Infantry Regiment, 2nd Infantry Division.

His regiment was quickly shipped off to the UK for specific training for the planned invasion of Normandy.

The Heroic Act

José's division landed in Normandy on the 7th of June, and he was soon one of hundreds of Allied soldiers wounded by the Axis' bombardment. Despite his wounds, he scoffed at the thought of being evacuated from the battlefield and fought on to contribute toward the Allies' successful invasion. It was months later, in December, that José's division had fought all the way through to Belgium and found themselves seemingly staring death in the face when German forces broke through Allied lines within the dense forestry of the Ardennes.

The Allied lines were vital in allowing them the continued benefit of the Belgian city of Antwerp, so the Germans devised a plan to split the lines and encircle four Allied armies with the goal of eventually forcing them into surrender.

The German plan nearly worked, and they were able to catch the Allies off-guard due to a combination of being focused on plans elsewhere, overconfidence, and bad weather that had grounded their air forces.

Another important factor was that the Allies were using the area primarily as a resting post, meaning that many of the soldiers there were tired and refueling before bigger battles to come. Little did they and José know that the Battle of the Bulge was coming to them.

On December 17, the Germans executed their plan with devastating effect.

At the time of the attack, José had been temporarily assigned to K Company 23rd Infantry Regiment so that he could support them with his machine gun. I'm sure that when that decision was made, no one could anticipate just how effective José and his machine gun would be.

He was away from his company and relaxing on a snowy patch of ground when José spotted German infantry and tanks storming toward them. Knowing that he had to take action, José used every bit of his 5-foot-5-inch, 130-pound frame to lug his heavy Browning machine gun—a gun that usually requires multiple men to operate it effectively—from his company's right flank across to its left and settled into a shallow hole. José had no cover above his waist and was in an incredibly vulnerable position, yet still, he stabbed the three legs of the gun's tripod into the icy dirt and funneled ammunition into the chamber.

José said a prayer to the Mexican monument, Basilica of Our Lady of Guadalupe, for protection before letting rip with every fiber of his being that day, expecting to be killed at any moment. To José, his life wasn't the immediate priority. His only goal was to give his company as much time as possible to withdraw to a more advantageous position.

With his bones and the gun held tightly within his hands, juddering viscously, José was still able to hold the heavy weapon steady enough to cut through the first ten of his casualties that day despite being targeted by a tank ominously approaching.

Suddenly, being swarmed by infantry rushing his company from the right-hand side, José pivoted sharply and prepared to engage. Before he could open fire once more, an artillery shell crashed into the ground, having missed him by mere yards.

José was shaken and disorientated. Yet, with his ears ringing and stinging, he was able to regain his composure and take another 25 lives before they could take those of his company.

Realizing that he was in danger of being outflanked, he dragged his weapon out of the dirt and through the forest to the far right of the enemy. He was met by the sight of his company being forced back, but they needed time to do so safely.

José was suddenly blown backward by a shell that took him off his feet. Once again, he was able to shake off his disorientation and defiantly stab the gun's tripod into the frozen forest floor. He tore into the enemy once more, firing for the mother that he'd lost, firing for the uncle that took him in, and firing for the beloved country that he called home.

He fired with such ferocity, in fact, that he was able to hold off the German horde for long enough that his company could withdraw safely. Only once he was satisfied that they had did he throw his gun over his back and sprint as fast as his tired legs would carry him to evade a hailstorm of small arms fire and reconvene with his company as they struggled to set up some form of defense.

They needed time, and José obliged once more.

He provided covering fire until he'd exhausted his very last shell, and then successfully fell back with the rest of his company.

José killed in excess of 100 enemy soldiers that day, and without him, Company K would have been completely obliterated and unable to contribute to the Allies' eventual victory in the Battle of the Bulge.

The Aftermath of the Act

When José returned home to the United States, he was met by a raucous reception in New York City and greeted by the mayor of the city.

He moved his family to San Antonio and began working with the Veterans Administration as his life away from the war started to take shape. Unfortunately, like many veterans, José struggled to acclimatize to life after the war and found himself re-enlisting in 1949.

He continued to serve the United States Army, including receiving accolades for his efforts throughout the Korean War, until his retirement in 1973. At the time of his retirement, he had achieved the rank of master sergeant.

José died in 2005 at the age of 94, one year after he'd lost his beloved wife with whom he'd spent 62 years. He was buried at the Fort Sam Houston National Cemetery in San Antonio, Texas.

A Lasting Legacy

José was awarded the Medal of Honor in June of 1945. His citation reads:

> On his own initiative, he carried his heavy machine gun from Company K's right flank to its left, in order to protect that flank, which was in danger of being overrun by advancing enemy infantry supported by tanks. Occupying a shallow hole offering no protection above the waist, he cut down a group of 10 Germans. Ignoring enemy fire from an advancing tank, he held his position and cut down 25 more enemy infantry attempting to turn his flank.
>
> Glancing to his right, he saw a large number of infantry swarming in from the front. Although dazed and shaken from enemy artillery fire which had crashed into the ground only a few yards away, he realized that his position soon would be outflanked. Again, alone, he carried his machine gun to a position to the right rear of the sector; enemy tanks and infantry were forcing a withdrawal. Blown over backwards by the concussion of enemy fire, he immediately reset his gun and continued his fire.
>
> Singlehanded he held off the German horde until he was satisfied his company had effected its retirement. Again he loaded his gun on his back and in a hail of small-arms fire he ran to a point where a few of his comrades were attempting to set up another defense

> against the onrushing enemy. He fired from this position until his ammunition was exhausted. Still carrying his gun, he fell back with his small group to Krinkelt. Sgt. López's gallantry and intrepidity, on seemingly suicidal missions in which he killed at least 100 of the enemy, were almost solely responsible for allowing Company K to avoid being enveloped, to withdraw successfully, and to give other forces coming up in support time to build a line which repelled the enemy drive. (Martin, 2020)

The United States weren't the only country to honor José, however, with Mexico's Mayor also bestowing their highest military award, La Condecoración del Mérito Militar, on him during a pilgrimage to the Basilica of Our Lady of Guadalupe in Mexico City—a monument representing the very Saint that José had prayed to for protection while at war.

José López was also awarded the following for his efforts with the United States Army (López, 2024):

- Combat Infantryman Badge with one star
- Bronze Star with one oak leaf cluster
- Army Good Conduct Medal with a bronze clasp and four loops
- Purple Heart
- Army Commendation Medal
- Army Defense Service Medal
- American Campaign Medal
- Army of Occupation Medal

- National Defense Service Medal
- European-African-Middle Eastern Campaign Medal
- World War II Victory Medal
- United Nations Korea Medal
- Korean War Service Medal
- Korean Service Medal with three Campaign stars

Texas has also named a city park, a street, and a middle school in José's honor. There is a statue proudly erected of him in Brownsville's Veterans Park.

José López stood tall in the face of ferocity to prevent the slaughter of Company K, ensuring their key contribution during the Battle of the Bulge.

Conclusion

By September 2, 1945, the world had been immeasurably changed and forever altered by the Second World War. While we hear about the wider battles, the moments of heroic generals, and the sacrifice of those in power, often the individual stories of heroes are lost within the carnage.

The preceding stories of heroism are merely a small sample of the many heroic actions taken throughout World War II. I've done my best to provide a cross-section of lesser-known examples but narrowing it down to such was an incredibly difficult task due to the sheer volume of American heroes who risked their lives for their country to ensure the Allies' victory.

I truly hope that this publication has gone some way to honoring those who were at risk of having their stories fade to time and that you are inspired to continue your research into some of these incredible Americans and continue their legacy.

Remember, every individual has the strength within to rise to the occasion. Thank you for reading; I hope to see you for the next in our *Heroes of World War II* series.

–Alex Viner.

References

Ackerman, C. (2021, February 19). *"I did not send for you" – John Fox and the Medal of Honor.* National Medal of Honor Museum. https://mohmuseum.org/john-fox-and-the-medal-of-honor/#:~:text=He%20was%20warned%20the%20coordinates

Aiken, D. (2001). *Doris Miller and his Navy Cross: A brief biography.* Archive. Today. https://archive.ph/20121209093049/http://www.pearlharborattacked.com/cgi-bin/IKONBOARDNEW312a/ikonboard.cgi#selection-37.1-37.51

Battle of Midway. (2019, April 30). Wikipedia; Wikimedia Foundation. https://en.wikipedia.org/wiki/Battle_of_Midway

Battle of the Bulge. (2018, December 16). Wikipedia. https://en.wikipedia.org/wiki/Battle_of_the_Bulge

Bill De Giulio. (2024). *Robert Wright and Kenneth Moore: An incredible D-Day story.* WanderWisdom. https://wanderwisdom.com/travel-destinations/Amazing-Untold-D-Day-Story

Bong -- Maj Richard Ira Bong. (n.d.). Air Force Historical Support Division. https://www.afhistory.af.mil/FAQs/Fact-Sheets/Article/639628/bong-maj-richard-ira-bong/

Brigit Katz. (2019, April 8). *How a spy known as the "Limping Lady" helped the Allies win WWII.* Smithsonian. https://www.smithsonianmag.com/history/how-spy-known-limping-lady-helped-allies-win-wwii-180971889/

Caltrider, M. (2022). *The most decorated officer in the history of the 82nd airborne laid to rest in Arlington.* Coffee or Die Magazine. https://coffeeordie.com/decorated-officer-82nd-airborne

Campbell, E. (2022). *Colleyville woman honors soldier who liberated her father from Nazi concentration camp.* Fort Werth Star-Telegram. https://www.star-telegram.com/news/local/community/northeast-tarrant/article265218901.html

Captain Charles L. Thomas. (n.d.). My Black History. https://www.myblackhistory.net/Charles_Thomas.htm

Charles L. Thomas. (2024, January 21). Wikipedia. https://en.wikipedia.org/wiki/Charles_L._Thomas

Charles Leroy Thomas. (n.d.). Congressional Medal of Honor Society. https://www.cmohs.org/recipients/charles-l-thomas

Colonel James Megellas. (n.d.). American Veterans Center. https://americanveteranscenter.org/2014/12/colonel-james-megellas/

Commander Ernest E. Evans: Down with the ship. (2021, November 18). VA News. https://news.va.gov/97081/commander-ernest-e-evans-down-with-the-ship/

Cook Third Class Doris Miller's Navy Cross citation. (2020). Public2.Nhhcaws.local. https://www.history.navy.mil/browse-by-topic/diversity/african-americans/miller/doris-millers-navy-cross-citation.html#:~:text=CITATION%3A%20%22For%20distinguished%20devotion%20to

Cowles, G. (2011). *Inside the list.* The New York Times. https://www.nytimes.com/2011/11/27/books/review/inside-the-list.html

Dawsey, J. (2023, February 13). *Recognition after a long wait: Ruben Rivers' Medal of Honor.* The National WWII Museum. https://www.nationalww2museum.org/war/articles/recognition-after-long-wait-ruben-rivers-medal-honor

Doris Miller. (2019, November 6). Wikipedia; Wikimedia Foundation. https://en.wikipedia.org/wiki/Doris_Miller

Douglas Albert Munro. (2024, February 12). Wikipedia. https://en.wikipedia.org/wiki/Douglas_Albert_Munro

Eagle Scout. (2024, June 1). Wikipedia. https://en.wikipedia.org/wiki/Eagle_Scout

Elder, G. (2016, October 27). *Faces of defense intelligence: Virginia Hall - the "limping lady."* Defense Intelligence Agency. https://www.dia.mil/News-Features/Articles/Article-View/Article/988284/faces-of-defense-intelligence-virginia-hall-the-limping-lady/

Ernest E. Evans. (2024, April 30). Wikipedia. https://en.wikipedia.org/wiki/Ernest_E._Evans#cite_note-USNA_Virtual_Memorial_Hall-1

Ernest Edwin "Chief" Evans. (n.d.). Congressional Medal of Honor Society. https://www.cmohs.org/recipients/ernest-edwin-chief-evans

Ernest Edwin Evans. (2021). Naval History and Heritage Command. https://www.history.navy.mil/research/library/research-guides/modern-biographical-files-ndl/modern-bios-e/evans-ernest-edwin.html

Eugene B. Fluckey. (2024, March 18). Wikipedia. https://en.wikipedia.org/wiki/Eugene_B._Fluckey

Eugene B. Fluckey quotes. (n.d.). Goodreads. https://www.goodreads.com/author/quotes/458959.Eugene_B_Fluckey#:~:text=Today%20we%20live%3B%20tomorrow%E2%80%94who

First Lieutenant Vernon J. Baker . (n.d.). BHA. https://www.myblackhistory.net/Vernon_Baker.htm

Florence Finch. (n.d.). U.S. National Park Service. https://www.nps.gov/articles/000/florence-finch.htm

Frank D. Peregory. (2024, February 10). Wikipedia. https://en.wikipedia.org/wiki/Frank_D._Peregory

Franklin Delano Roosevelt Memorial. (2015). U.S. National Park Service. https://www.nps.gov/frde/learn/photosmultimedia/q

uotations.htm#:~:text=%22More%20than%20an%20end%20to

George Watson. (n.d.). National Park Service. https://www.nps.gov/people/georgewatson.htm

George Watson (Medal of Honor). (2024, February 10). Wikipedia. https://en.wikipedia.org/wiki/George_Watson_(Medal_of_Honor)#cite_note-5

Giovanni, J. (2007). What's a girl to do when a battle lands in her lap? *The New York Times Magazine*, 68–71.

Haskew, M. (2008). *Segregation in the U.S. Military: Ruben Rivers.* Warfare History Network. https://warfarehistorynetwork.com/article/segregation-in-the-u-s-military-ruben-rivers/

He fought... keeps mop. (1942, July 25). *New Pittsburgh Courier*, 12. https://www.newspapers.com/article/new-pittsburgh-courier-he-fought-keep/17249167/

Hillenbr, L. (2010, December 20). *The Great Zamperini.* Runner's World. https://www.runnersworld.com/races-places/a20839124/the-great-louie-zamperinis-running-story/

Hoarn, S. (2014). *Pfc. Leo J. Powers - unlikely Medal of Honor recipient during Battle of Monte Cassino.* Defense Media Network. https://www.defensemedianetwork.com/stories/pfc-leo-s-powers-unsung-medal-of-honor-recipient/

Hoeferlin, C. (2014). *Sergeant John Basilone.* MarineParents.com®.

https://marineparents.com/marinecorps/john-basilone.asp#:~:text=Navy%20Cross%20Citation%3A

Hogfeldt, V. (2019). *Soderman a hero for the ages.* West Haven Voice. https://westhavenvoice.com/soderman-a-hero-for-the-ages/

I'm staying with my boys... quotes. (n.d.). Goodreads https://www.goodreads.com/work/quotes/758075-i-m-staying-with-my-boys-the-heroic-life-of-sgt-john-basilone-usm

"In Their Own Words" - Phil Rasmussen. (2021). DVIDS. https://www.dvidshub.net/video/824204/their-own-words-phil-rasmussen

James Megellas. (n.d.). Sightline Media Group. https://valor.militarytimes.com/hero/22449

James Megellas. (2024, February 26). Wikipedia. https://en.wikipedia.org/wiki/James_Megellas

Jane Kendeigh. (2020, December 28). Wikipedia. https://en.wikipedia.org/wiki/Jane_Kendeigh

John Basilone. (2020, November 14). Wikipedia. https://en.wikipedia.org/wiki/John_Basilone

John R. Fox. (n.d.). National Park Service. https://www.nps.gov/people/johnfox.htm

John R. Fox. (2019, April 9). Wikipedia; Wikimedia Foundation. https://en.wikipedia.org/wiki/John_R._Fox

John Robert Fox. (n.d.). Congressional Medal of Honor Society. https://www.cmohs.org/recipients/john-r-fox

John R. Fox facts for kids. (n.d.). Kiddle. https://kids.kiddle.co/John_R._Fox

John William Finn. (2010). Naval History and Heritage Command. https://www.history.navy.mil/research/library/research-guides/modern-biographical-files-ndl/modern-bios-f/finn-john-william.html

John William Finn. (2012). Navylog.navymemorial.org. https://navylog.navymemorial.org/finn-john-0

John William Finn. (2023, March 28). Wikipedia. https://en.wikipedia.org/wiki/John_William_Finn

Jose M. Lopez. (2001). Voces Oral History Center. https://voces.moody.utexas.edu/collections/stories/jose-m-lopez#:~:text=%22We%20fought%20very%20hard%20against

José M. López. (2024, May 15). Wikipedia. https://en.wikipedia.org/wiki/Jos%C3%A9_M._L%C3%B3pez

Kaeding, D. (2024, May 24). *Hidden in the jungle, team finds fighter plane flown by ace pilot Richard Bong.* Wisconsin Public Radio. https://www.wpr.org/news/hidden-in-the-jungle-team-finds-fighter-plane-flown-by-ace-pilot-richard-bong

Kenney, G., C. (1949). *General Kenney reports: A personal history of the Pacific War* (pp. 3–6). DIANE Publishing.

Kutch, A. (n.d.). *Ever forward: The story of Frank Peregory, Medal of Honor recipient.* https://nebula.wsimg.com/37b3de4fb7e4511364b68be00fb5c5ad?AccessKeyId=D3E362E4074E454B6228&disposition=0&alloworigin=1

Lange, K. (2018). *Medal of Honor Monday: Army Pfc. William A. Soderman.* U.S. Department of Defense. https://www.defense.gov/News/Feature-Stories/story/Article/1712872/medal-of-honor-monday-army-pfc-william-a-soderman/

Lange, K. (2020). *Medal of Honor Monday: Army Maj. Charles L. Thomas.* U.S. Department of Defense. https://www.defense.gov/News/Feature-Stories/story/Article/2440776/medal-of-honor-monday-army-maj-charles-l-thomas/

Lange, K. (2021). *Medal of Honor Monday: Navy Cmdr. Ernest E. Evans.* U.S. Department of Defense. https://www.defense.gov/News/Feature-Stories/story/Article/2572567/medal-of-honor-monday-navy-cmdr-ernest e evans/#:~:text=At%20the%20ship%27s%20commissioning%20in

Lange, K. (2022). *Medal of Honor Monday: Army Pvt. Nicholas Minue.* U.S. Department of Defense. https://www.defense.gov/News/Feature-Stories/Story/Article/3022931/medal-of-honor-monday-army-pvt-nicholas-minue/

Lee Miller. (2019, December 17). Wikipedia; Wikimedia Foundation. https://en.wikipedia.org/wiki/Lee_Miller

Lee Miller's Second World War. (n.d.). Imperial War Museums. https://www.iwm.org.uk/history/lee-millers-second-world-war

Lengel, E. (2020, July 24). *Major Charles L. Thomas and the 614th tank destroyer battalion.* The National WWII Museum. https://www.nationalww2museum.org/war/articles/614th-tank-destroyer-battalion-climbach-1944

Lieutenant John William Finn, USN, (1909-2010). (2012, December 11). Web.archive.org. https://web.archive.org/web/20121211105556/http://www.history.navy.mil/photos/pers-us/uspers-f/j-finn.htm

Louis Zamperini. (2019, May 22). Wikipedia; Wikimedia Foundation. https://en.wikipedia.org/wiki/Louis_Zamperini

Lt Col Philip M. Rasmussen. (n.d.). Military Hall of Honor. https://militaryhallofhonor.com/honoree-record.php?id=2987

McLellan, D. (2002, June 2). *Ruby Bradley, 94; army nurse was "Angel in Fatigues" for POWs.* Los Angeles Times. https://www.latimes.com/archives/la-xpm-2002-jun-02-me-bradley2-story.html

Medal of Honor recipients. (2008, June 16). Web.archive.org. https://web.archive.org/web/20080616211621/http://www.history.army.mil/html/moh/wwII-a-f.html

Medal of Honor recipients - World War II (A-F). (2008, June 16). Web.archive.org.

https://web.archive.org/web/20080616211621/http://www.history.army.mil/html/moh/wwII-a-f.html

Megellas, J. (2007). *All the way to Berlin*. Presidio Press.

Mendoza, J. (2019, December 7). *On Dec. 7, 1941, a shipyard worker and his son jumped into action to save lives*. Hawaii News Now. https://www.hawaiinewsnow.com/2019/12/07/dec-shipyard-worker-his-son-jumped-into-action-save-lives/

Mildred Harnack. (n.d.). The German Resistance Memorial Center. https://www.gdw-berlin.de/en/recess/biographies/index_of_persons/biographie/view-bio/mildred-harnack/?no_cache=1

Mildred Harnack. (2022, October 16). Wikipedia. https://en.wikipedia.org/wiki/Mildred_Harnack

Military Aviation Museum. (2021). *Ace of aces: The story of Richard Bong*. YouTube. https://www.youtube.com/watch?v=Tdj-NUrAQiw

Miller, Doris. (2017, June 6). Naval History and Heritage Command. https://www.history.navy.mil/research/histories/biographies-list/bios-m/miller-doris.html

Minister of War (Netherlands). (2023, October 29). Wikipedia. https://en.wikipedia.org/wiki/Minister_of_War_(Netherlands)

Momodu, S. (2021, January 19). *Ruben Rivers (1921-1944)*. Black Past. https://www.blackpast.org/african-american-history/ruben-rivers-1921-1944/

Morse, H. (1999). *George Walters - Pearl Harbor crane operator.* Submarine Sailor. http://www.submarinesailor.com/biography/georgewalters/

Myre, G. (2019, April 18). *"A woman of no importance" finally gets her due.* NPR. https://www.npr.org/2019/04/18/711356336/a-woman-of-no-importance-finally-gets-her-due

Nicholas Minue. (2024, March 18). Wikipedia. https://en.wikipedia.org/wiki/Nicholas_Minue

Norman, E. M. (2013). *We band of angels: The untold story of American nurses trapped on Bataan* (p. 317). Random House.

Norman Jack Kleiss. (n.d.). Sightline Media Group. https://valor.militarytimes.com/hero/21311

Norman Kleiss. (2024, January 27). Wikipedia. https://en.wikipedia.org/wiki/Norman_Kleiss

Oliver, M. (2005, May 18). *Jose M. Lopez, 94; Battle of the Bulge hero killed 100 German soldiers.* Los Angeles Times. https://www.latimes.com/archives/la-xpm-2005-may-18-me-joselopezobit18-story.html

Olsen, K. (2010, July 16). *World War II hero Vernon Baker dies.* Web.archive.org. https://web.archive.org/web/20100716221300/http://www.spokesman.com/stories/2010/jul/14/world-war-ii-hero-vernon-baker-dies/

Philip Rasmussen. (n.d.). Sightline Media Group. https://valor.militarytimes.com/hero/49417

Phil Rasmussen. (2019, September 28). Wikipedia; Wikimedia Foundation. https://en.wikipedia.org/wiki/Phil_Rasmussen

Platoon Sergeant Ruben Rivers and the 761st tank battalion. (2020). The National WWII Museum. https://www.nationalww2museum.org/war/articles/761st-tank-battalion-guebling-1944

Private George Watson. (n.d.). The National World War II Museum. https://mymemorialday.org/remember/watson.php

Private George Watson's Medal of Honor. (2022). The National WWII Museum | New Orleans. https://www.nationalww2museum.org/war/articles/private-george-watsons-medal-honor

Purnell, S. (2019). *A Woman of* no i*mportance*. Hachette UK.

Quotes by Lee Miller. (n.d.). PhotoQuotes. https://photoquotes.com/quote/nearly-all-the-photographs-i-ever-took-have-disapp

Rasmussen, P. (2021, November 9). *The pajama pilot over Pearl Harbor*. HistoryNet. https://www.historynet.com/the-pajama-pilot-over-pearl-harbor/

Recognition after a long wait: Ruben R*ivers' medal of honor*. (2023, February 13). The National WWII Museum | New Orleans. https://www.nationalww2museum.org/war/articles/re

cognition-after-long-wait-ruben-rivers-medal-honor#:~:text=Staff%20Sergeant%20Rivers%2C%20however%2C%20radioed

Richard Bong. (2023, April 8). Wikipedia. https://en.wikipedia.org/wiki/Richard_Bong

Richard Bong Ace of Aces. (n.d.). Richard Bong. https://richardbong.weebly.com/awards.html

Richard Ira "Bing" Bong. (n.d.). Acesofww2.com. https://acesofww2.com/USA/aces/bong/#:~:text=And%20if%20I%20was%20over

Roberts, S. (2017, April 28). Florence Finch, unsung war hero who took on Japanese, dies at 101. *The New York Times.* https://www.nytimes.com/2017/04/28/us/florence-finch-dead-coast-guard-war-hero.html

Roos, D. (2023, March 21). *A Wisconsin woman led a German resistance that enraged Hitler.* HowStuffWorks. https://history.howstuffworks.com/historical-figures/mildred-harnack.htm

Rossiter, M. L. (1986). *Women in the resistance* (pp. 196–197). Greenwood.

Ruben Rivers. (n.d.-a). National Park Service. https://www.nps.gov/people/rubenrivers.htm

Ruben Rivers. (n.d.-b). Liberation Route Europe. https://www.liberationroute.com/stories/12/ruben-rivers

Ruben Rivers. (2022, September 6). Wikipedia. https://en.wikipedia.org/wiki/Ruben_Rivers

Ruby Bradley. (2019, February 27). Wikipedia; Wikimedia Foundation. https://en.wikipedia.org/wiki/Ruby_Bradley

Saving oneself or saving others: Pvt. George Watson. (2022). American Battle Monuments Commission. https://www.abmc.gov/news-events/news/saving-oneself-or-saving-others-pvt-george-watson

SECNAV names ship after World War II hero, Medal of Honor recipient Ernest E. Evans. (2023). United States Navy. https://www.navy.mil/Press-Office/Press-Releases/display-pressreleases/Article/3590215/secnav-names-ship-after-world-war-ii-hero-medal-of-honor-recipient-ernest-e-eva/

Smith, S. (2023, November 9). *Nurse Ruby Bradley Rose to be most decorated woman in U.S. Army*. Investor's Business Daily. https://www.investors.com/news/management/leaders-and-success/ruby-bradley-rose-to-be-most-decorated-woman-in-us-army-history/

Sobocinski, A. (2013). *Angels of the airfields: Navy air evacuation nurses of World War II* . Naval Historical Foundation. https://navyhistory.org/2013/05/angels-of-the-airfields-navy-air-evacuation-nurses-ww2/#:~:text=As%20ENS%20Jane%20Kendeigh%20would

Stories of sacrifice. (n.d.). Congressional Medal of Honor Society. https://www.cmohs.org/recipients/nicholas-minue

Street, K. (2016). *Ruby Grace Bradley.* Prezi. https://prezi.com/n9wjsjikdps2/ruby-grace-bradley/

tara. (2022a, April 7). *This day in history: The first Navy flight nurse.* Taraross. https://www.taraross.com/post/tdih-jane-kendeigh

tara. (2022b, June 13). *This day in history: George Watson's Medal of Honor.* Taraross. https://www.taraross.com/post/tdih-george-watson-moh

tara. (2023, April 17). *This day in history: Charles Thomas's bravery in France.* Taraross. https://www.taraross.com/post/tdih-charles-l-thomas-moh

The top 10 of everything in 2010. (2010). Time. https://web.archive.org/web/20101212222713/http://www.time.com/time/specials/packages/completelist/0,29569,2035319,00.html

The words of war. (2018, July 17). The National WWII Museum | New Orleans. https://www.nationalww2museum.org/war/articles/words-war-28

Thiesen, W. (2022). *The long blue line: Florence Finch—Asian-American SPAR and FRC namesake dons uniform 75 years ago!* United States Coast Guard. https://www.history.uscg.mil/Research/THE-LONG-BLUE-LINE/Article/2925497/the-long-blue-line-florence-finchasian-american-spar-and-frc-namesake-dons-unif/

Unbroken: Chapters 10 – 11. (n.d.). SparkNotes. https://www.sparknotes.com/lit/unbroken/section6/

Vernon Baker. (n.d.). National Park Service. https://www.nps.gov/people/vernonbaker.htm#:~:text=Vernon%20Baker%27s%20Medal%20of%20Honor

Vernon Baker. (2021, February 15). Wikipedia. https://en.wikipedia.org/wiki/Vernon_Baker

Villa, A. (2021, March 19). *Photographer Lee Miller's subversive career took her from Vogue to war-torn Germany.* Art in America. https://www.artnews.com/feature/lee-miller-photography-vogue-man-ray-1234587240/

Virginia Hall. (n.d.). Sightline Media Group. https://valor.militarytimes.com/hero/22199

Virginia Hall. (2024, March 27). Wikipedia. https://en.wikipedia.org/wiki/Virginia_Hall#cite_note-WaPo-47

William A. Soderman. (2024, February 14). Wikipedia. https://en.wikipedia.org/wiki/William_A._Soderman

William Wilbur. (n.d.). The Hall of Valor Project. https://valor.militarytimes.com/hero/3292#22531

William H. Wilbur. (2023, February 17). Wikipedia. https://en.wikipedia.org/wiki/William_H._Wilbur

World War II at 75: The women at Iwo Jima. (2020, April 3). Submarine Force Library & Association. https://ussnautilus.org/world-war-ii-at-75-the-women-at-iwo-jima/

World War II Medal of Honor recipient's heroism remembered 70 years later. (2013, April 28). American Battle Monuments Commission. https://www.abmc.gov/news-events/news/world-war-ii-medal-honor-recipient%E2%80%99s-heroism-remembered-70-years-later

WWII 75: Marching to victory. (2020, September 4). Truman Library Institute. https://www.trumanlibraryinstitute.org/wwii-75-marching-victory-23/

Zamperini, Louis Silvie "Louie." (n.d.). Traces of War. https://www.tracesofwar.com/persons/68223/Zamperini-Louis-Silvie-Louie.htm

Image References

Congressional Medal of Honor Society (n.d.) *Leo J. Powers* [image]. Congressional Medal of Honor Society. https://www.cmohs.org/recipients/leo-j-powers

Congressional Medal of Honor Society (n.d.) *Nicholas Minue* [image]. Congressional Medal of Honor Society. https://www.cmohs.org/recip

The book cover has been designed using assets from Freepik.com

Made in United States
North Haven, CT
19 January 2025

64636734R00165